ABRAHAMIC
FAITHS: IN THE ERA OF GLOBALIZATION

Dr. Mohiuddin Waseem

Dedications

To my daughters Affaf, Zaynah, and Hadiyah, who are the happiness in my life.

Acknowledgments

I would like to begin by thanking my parents, Dr. Waheeduddin and Mrs. Hameeda Akhtar, who always stressed the importance of acquiring knowledge and helped me in every possible way to achieve this goal. I am also thankful to my maternal grand-parents, Mr. Mirza Humayun Akhtar and Mrs. Zubaida Sultan, both from the lineage of the Mogul emperors of India, who inculcated in me a zest for religious studies and were the first during my childhood to make me recite in a ceremony these few verses from the Holy Quran, "Read in the name of thy Lord and Cherisher who created" (Holy Quran 96:1).

My wife, Ambareen Khan, deserves special thanks from the depths of my heart for editing the articles and for her constant support and encouragement during the preparation of this book.

I also would like to thank my longtime friend Dr. Amir Burney for providing me the cover photograph for this book, which perfectly complements the title. The photograph shows the pillars and arches of Shah Jahan Mosque, located in Thatta, an ancient city of the Indus valley, Pakistan. The mosque was built during the reign of Mogul Emperor Shah Jahan in 1647. Historically, this mosque is famous for sheer number of domes it contains — over one hundred, the largest number of domes in a mosque in the world. In its construction the mosque builders employed the science of acoustics with such perfection that the Imam's voice can reach every corner of the mosque without the help of a loudspeaker.

My daughter Affaf needs special thanks for providing me her creative art for the book's back cover.

Last, but definitely not least, I want to thank my uncle Mirza Asad Humayun, professor of history, for sharing with me his insight on many crucial historic events, which definitely influenced my understanding on the topics discussed in this book.

"At the recitation ceremony of the Holy Quran with my maternal grandmother Zubaida Sultan (left), my aunt Farnaz (right) and my mother Hameeda Akhtar (center)".

About The Author

Dr. Mohiuddin Waseem is a consultant physician specializing in internal medicine and chronic wound care. He graduated from Dow Medical College, Karachi, Pakistan, and received his post graduate training at Cook County Hospital, Chicago, Illinois. He is a diplomate of the American Board of Internal Medicine, a fellow of the American College of Physicians, and a certified wound specialist from American Board of Wound Management. He belongs to an educated family and traces his ancestry back to Abu Bakar Siddiq, the companion of Prophet Mohammad. He is married and blessed with three daughters. He can be reached at the following e-mail address:

-AbrahamicFaiths@hotmail.com

Preface

This is a unique and exciting time to live. Globalization has brought people of different faiths and civilizations closer to each other, to the extent that one can appreciate how small the world has become in the last few decades. In ancient times it took over three weeks for the news of Julius Caesar's assassination to reach Jerusalem. Today, with the advent of mass communication tools, people witness live events as they unfold. Though globalization as a whole has been beneficial to humanity in improving the social interaction of different cultures and civilizations, the flip side of the coin is its tendency to unmask and escalate intercultural and interreligious conflicts. The events of 9/11exemplified this: the attack on the World Trade Center and Pentagon were seen as the epitome of the age-old conflict between Islam and Christianity. Just like the terrorists who were wrong to use the Holy Quran to justify their acts, the opponents also referred to out of context Quranic verses to show its volatile preaching; at least here both were in agreement that Islam preaches extremism. And just like Christianity, which once was looked upon with suspicion after the fire of Rome during Emperor Nero's reign, Islam, too, had to go through a period of tough scrutiny in the post 9/11 era.

During my study of the Abrahamic faiths I learned that Islam, Christianity, and Judaism share a unanimous under-standing that God created the heavens and earth, and every-thing therein, for his worship alone. To this end humans were expected to play an important role and that was to disseminate the message of monotheism. From the very beginning their volatile nature was appreciated, but scripture tells us that humans are designed to preserve God's doing in the world and not to destroy it. The Holy Bible puts this belief beautifully by saying "God created man in his image" (Gen.1:27), a metaphoric likeness with God the Creator and the Preserver. In the Holy Quran God rebuked the Angels in a discourse when they argued that "Man will cause mischief in the world and shed blood" by saying, "You do not know what I know" (Holy Quran 2: 30). If we are the chosen people of God, as we all claim we are then we need to do such preserving acts that will make us worthy of God's trust and work for the betterment of humanity.

I would like to reiterate that it is not my idea, but the Quranic command to all Muslims to look for common grounds with other religions. The Holy Quran says, "O People of the Scripture (Jews and Christians), Come to common terms between us and you: that we shall worship none but God, and that we shall ascribe no partners unto Him, and that none of us shall take others for lords beside God. And if they turn away, then say: Bear witness that we are they who have surrendered (unto Him)" (Holy Quran 3:64).

We should remember that this message of monotheism is not at all new to our religious cousins in Abrahamic faiths — Jews and Christians — who were the forebears of Divine revelations in the form of the Old and New Testament respectively, as our Christian brethren refer to it, before it was finally given to Prophet Mohammad as the Holy Quran, the Last and Final Testament. In a world of varied religious ideologies the only thing that can bring these different Abrahamic faiths closer is a quest for true monotheism and it is superfluous to say that in this regard the Holy Quran has already made its call.

Lastly, I want to thank my younger brother Dr. Naseemuddin Khurram for co-authoring with me two of the articles, "Graves and Ancestor Worship in Abrahamic Faiths" and "Mehdi Revealed". All the articles compiled in this book were written over the last many years and cover interfaith issues with the intention to improve understanding between the followers of the Abrahamic faiths.

I am confident you'll have an interesting read.

Dr. Mohiuddin Waseem

www.AbrahamicFaiths.net

Interfaith tolerance as envisioned by my daughter Affaf Waseem

Chapters

1. The Legacy of Prophet Abraham (PBUH)

From his homeland in Babylon, some four thousand years ago, Prophet Abraham, peace be upon him (PBUH), set out on a journey to Palestine, Egypt, and Arabia. His legacy is very important as it is the difference in the interpretation of this journey, which gave birth to the three most important religions — Islam, Christianity, and Judaism — and provides the basis for the deep-seated rift between the followers of these monotheistic religions. A brief review is in order as no other event in human history has so profoundly influenced the course of history as this one.

In the Judeo-Christian traditions his Hebrew name, Abraham, rightly means "father of many nations" (Gen.17:5). The biblical account of Abraham moves from Mesopotamia to Palestine then to Egypt and finally back to Palestine. He is portrayed as a member of a family associated with city life in Southern Babylon, moving to Haran (Southern Turkey) and finally to Canaan (Palestine), where God promised that Abraham's descendants would own a certain land (Gen.12:1–9) though the reason for this divine favor is never explained. Famine forced Abraham to Egypt where a tyrant Pharaoh of that time took Abraham's wife Sarah, whom Abraham had declared was his sister, into captivity. Discovering the truth later on, Pharaoh released Sarah and sent Abraham and Sarah away with all the wealth Abraham had acquired over the years (Gen.12:10–12).

Back again in Salam (Jerusalem), Abraham meets the King-Priest to whom he paid a tithe (Gen.14), suggesting the existence of other monotheistic faiths at that time. Childless Sarah gave Abraham her Egyptian maid Hagar to produce a son, who when born was named Ishmael, which means God heard (Gen.16). Thirteen years later Sarah, too, bore a son, Isaac, who would receive the covenant with God, whereas Ishmael received a separate promise of many descendants (Gen.17).[1] A few years after Isaac's birth, Hagar and Ishmael were sent away to wander in the desert, where the divine provision protected them (Gen. 21:1–20). Throughout his career Abraham built many alters at different places and offered sacrifices, thereby displaying his devotion to God Almighty (Gen.12:7–8 and 13:4), but it is his political side that interested biblical writers the most. Therefore, though it was Abraham's grandson Jacob (through Isaac) who gave his name to Israel and fathered the twelve tribes, Abraham was regarded as the nation's progenitor (Exod. 2:24 and 4:5). Years later, Israel's claim to Canaan rested on the promises made to Abraham because the God worshiped by Israel was preeminently the God of Abraham, so to speak (Exod. 3:6, 15; 1 Kings 18:36).

In contrast to the biblical account of Abraham's political legacy, the Islamic tradition addresses primarily the spiritual side of this mighty prophet. In the Holy Quran Abraham's name is mentioned sixty-nine times and he is counted among the five great resolute and steadfast prophets, including Noah, Moses, Jesus, and Mohammad (peace be upon them all) (Holy Quran 33:7). His story is one of great sacrifices and complete submission to God Almighty. Going through tremendous trials and sacrifices for the sake of God alone, he was elevated in rank for the leadership of humanity. The Holy Quran says, "And (remember) when the Lord of Abraham tried him with (certain) Commands[2], which he fulfilled. He (God) said (to him), "Verily,

I am going to make you an Imam (a leader) for mankind (to follow you)". Abraham said, "And also (Imams) from my off-spring!" God answered, "My Covenant includes not Zalimun (polytheists and wrong-doers)" (Holy Quran 2:124).

It is important to realize that throughout his ministry Abraham's arguments to his adversaries always rested on intellectual reasoning and rational grounds. Because his father was an idol maker it is safe to assume that Abraham belonged to a priestly family and was well aware of the pseudo-science of astrology and the other superstitions of his people. Therefore, with the help of God-given logic alone he was able to refute the falsehood of polytheists. The Holy Quran presents his argument to the star worshippers in an allegorical way.

> We showed Abraham the power and the laws of the heavens and the earth that he might (with understanding) have certitude. When the night fell he saw a star, he said "This is my Lord." But when it set, he said "I love not those that set." When he saw the moon rising in splendor he said "This is my Lord," but when the moon set he said "Unless my Lord guides me I shall surely be among those who go astray." When he saw the sun rising in splendor he said "This is my Lord; this is the greatest (of all)." But when the sun set he said "O my people! I am (now) free from your (guilt) of giving partners to God. (Holy Quran 6:75–78)

In another place to make a point to the idol worshippers "he broke their (idols) all to pieces but left the biggest of them so that they might turn (and address themselves) to"; they said "Who has done this to our gods? He must indeed be some man of impiety!" Abraham suggested they inquire from the idols "if they can speak" and thus settled the argument in his favor when his adversaries admitted, "Surely we are the ones in the wrong" (Holy Quran 21: 51–64).

It was because of his monotheistic message that he was abandoned by his parents, relatives, and friends, thrown in the fire that was meant to burn him alive (Holy Quran 21:68–69), and finally exiled by the king of the country whose claim of divinity was refuted by Abraham when he asked him if he could make the sun rise from the west. (Holy Quran 2:258). Abraham survived all these trials and stood firm as a rock for the sake of truth.

While in exile he traveled far and wide in various parts of the known world of that time calling people to the path of God. But he still had to face another momentous trial from his Lord. After he was blessed with a son at an old age, he had to leave this son, Ishmael, and his wife Hagar in the barren desolate of Bakka (Makkah) valley on God's command. The recent discovery of the "Dead Sea Scrolls" of the Essene community, a Jewish sect belonging to first century BCE Palestine, describes Abraham's travel east to the Euphrates and the Persian Gulf region, then around the coast of Arabia to the Red Sea, and finally to the Sinai desert and then to his home (Geza Vermes, *The Complete Dead Sea Scrolls*, Genesis Apocryphon 448–459). Abraham's awareness of the Arabian Peninsula suggests the possibility that the "desert" where, according to the Bible, Hagar and Ishmael wandered was in fact the Arabian desert of the Makkah region as has been claimed by the Muslims all along.

It was in Makkah that God gave a final test to him and ordered him to sacrifice the only son he had at that time (Ishmael). Abraham was successful in this test, too, but before

"On the occasion of Hajj 2008"

he could slaughter him with his own hands God called out, "O Abraham! Thou hast already fulfilled the vision! This was indeed a manifest trial" (Holy Quran 37:100–113). Satisfied with Abraham's complete submission and profound love, God ransomed Ishmael with a sacrificial animal. It is in commemoration of this event that animals are sacrificed during the Hajj, the yearly Muslim journey to Makkah, and by Muslims all over the world on the occasion of Eid-ul-Adha.

To the Muslim mind Prophet Abraham left behind a legacy of a true monotheistic religion for the sake of God Almighty. The Holy Quran says:

> And who turns away from the religion of Abraham except him who befools himself? We chose him and rendered pure in this world, and in the hereafter he is in the ranks of the righteous. When his Lord said to him: 'Submit to me' and he said: 'I submit my will to the Lord of the worlds'. And this was the legacy that Abraham left to his sons and so did Jacob; "O my sons! God has chosen the religion (faith) for you, so die not except in the state of submission." Were you witnesses when death came to Jacob? When he said to his sons: "What will you worship after me?" They said: "We shall worship your God; the God of your fathers Abraham, Ishmael and Isaac, the one (true) God; and to Him will we submit. (Holy Quran 2:130–133)

Notes:

1. Here it is logical to inquire why God chose Isaac as the principal heir of the covenant and gave Ishmael an inferior package. To this query no satisfactory answer can be found in the Bible. The Bible also tells us that after Sarah's demise "Abraham took a (third) wife whose name was Kethura. She bore him Zimran, Jokshan, Medan, Midian, Ishbak, and Shuah" (Gen. 25:1-2). Surprisingly, these children did not get anything from God at all, but only a few gifts that Abraham gave to the "sons of his concubines" (Gen. 25:6).

To understand the background of this apparent injustice you need to keep in mind that Judaism evolved in the tribal environment of the ancient Middle East where every pagan tribe and clan had its own god, therefore God (YHWH) of the Bible is shown imparting favoritism toward a certain people of interest, not necessarily for the sake of monotheism, but for the glory of a tribe: in this case, none else but Bani Israel itself. I have reason to believe that both Ishmael and Isaac had a normal brotherly relationship and like all young boys they too spent time playing together (Gen. 21:9–10) and in their adult age, upon their father's demise, buried him together (Gen. 25:9). But during the course of history later biblical writers introduced into the Bible a story that was meant to cater to their own vested interests. The following abridged verses are taken from the Hebrew Bible, which form the bedrock of the Jewish claim for their chosen status (*The Torah, A Modern Commentary*, Union of American Hebrew Congregations, New York, 1981). Please review it and notice the sequence of events.

1. "On that day the Lord made a covenant with Abram (Abraham), saying, "To your offspring I give this land, from the river of Egypt to the great river, the river Euphrates…" (Gen. 15:18)

2. Next, in Chapter 16, we are told that Abram's wife Sarai (Sarah) "had borne him no children" and Sarai said to Abram, "Look, the Lord has kept me from bearing. Consort with my maid; perhaps I shall have a son through her." And Abram heeded Sarai's request, so "Sarai, Abram's wife, took her maid, Hagar the Egyptian…after Abram had dwelt in the land of Canaan ten years…and gave her to her husband Abram as concubine." Finally "Hagar bore a son to Abram, and Abram gave the son that Hagar bore him the name Ishmael. Abram was eighty-six years old when Hagar bore Ishmael to Abram.

The name Ishmael means "God heeds" and from the above account it should be clear that it was Sarah's prayer that was answered, and most likely she must have taken good care of Hagar during her pregnancy and afterwards, and might have suggested the name herself.

3. Chapter 17 of Genesis starts by telling us that

> When Abram was ninety-nine years old, the Lord appeared to Abram and said to him…I will establish My covenant between Me and you, And I will make you exceedingly numerous…I will maintain My covenant between Me and you, and your offspring to come, as an everlasting covenant throughout the ages, to be God to you and to your offspring to come. I give the land you sojourn in to you and your offspring to come, all the land of Canaan, as an everlasting possession. I will be their God…Such shall be the covenant between Me and you and your offspring to follow which you shall keep: every male among you shall be circumcised. You shall circumcise the flesh of your foreskin, and that shall be the sign of the covenant between Me and you…As for your wife Sarai…I will bless her; indeed, I will give you a son by her. I will bless her so that she shall give rise to nations; rulers of people shall issue from her…As for Ishmael, I have heeded you. I hereby bless him. I will make him fertile and exceeding numerous. He shall be the father of twelve chieftains, and I will make of him a great nation. But My covenant I will maintain with Isaac, whom Sarah shall bear to you at this season next year…Then Abraham took his son Ishmael, and all his home born slaves and all those he had bought, every male in Abraham's household, and he circumcised the flesh of their foreskin on that very day, as God had spoken to him.

It should be clear from the above account that the mark of the covenant was circumcision and the first son of Abraham who entered into it was Ishmael himself and therefore excluding Ishmael and his descendants from the covenant is not justifiable. Most Judeo-Christian scholars are of the opinion that as Ishmael was born to a concubine he had certain legal rights but was not eligible for inheritance, which was the prevalent understanding among the pagans of the ancient world. But the scripture tells us that this kind of ideology was alien to ancient Israelites of Middle East, and in their culture even a slave-girl and her children had the same rights as any "certified" wife and her children had. The evidence you will find in the same book of Genesis, Chapter 21:9-10 where it reads, "Sarah saw the son (Ishmael), whom Hagar the Egyptian had borne to Abraham, playing (with Isaac). She said to Abraham, "cast out that slave-woman and her son, for the son of that slave shall not share in the inheritance with my son Isaac." It is important to note that the ancient Jewish editors didn't take comfort in Greco-Roman principles of inheritance and they knew that they had to do something more, maybe "cast someone out" to deny the legal inheritance. Sarah's fear of shared inheritance, in itself, also points toward the contrary.

Someone might rightly point out the explicit statement in which God preferentially "named" Isaac as the heir of the covenant. In my opinion those passages were deliberately introduced into the text "to keep the record straight"; especially during the period of Babylonian exile of Bani Israel, in the sixth century BCE, when, according to current biblical scholarship most of the Pentateuch (Torah) was edited (Introduction To The Old Testament: *The New Oxford Annotated Bible*, RSV 27). In fact, those were the days when the Ishmaelite emerged as an impressive force and started to shape the political environment of Ancient Middle East, especially between the seventh and the fifth century BCE. (*The Anchor Bible Dictionary*: Vol. 3:519).

Precisely for this reason the Holy Quran says "O People of the Book [Jews and Christians]! Exceed not in your religion the bounds [of what is proper], trespassing beyond the truth, nor follow the vein desires of people who went wrong in times gone by, who mislead many, and strayed [themselves] from the even way" (Holy Quran 5:80).

2. Ibn Abbas on the exegesis of the verse "And [remember] when the Lord of Abraham tried him with [certain] Commands, which he fulfilled" says that God tested Abraham by Taharah (cleanliness and purity); which included five kinds for the head and five kinds for the rest of the body. The

five kinds of Taharah for the head were (1) clipping of moustache, (2) rinsing the mouth, (3) cleaning the teeth, (4) rinsing the nose, and (5) combing the hair. For the body, the Taharah included (1) clipping nails, (2) shaving the private parts, (3) circumcision, (4) removing hair from the armpits, and (5) cleaning oneself with water after passing stool or urine (Ibn Kahtir, *Stories of the Prophets*, 178).

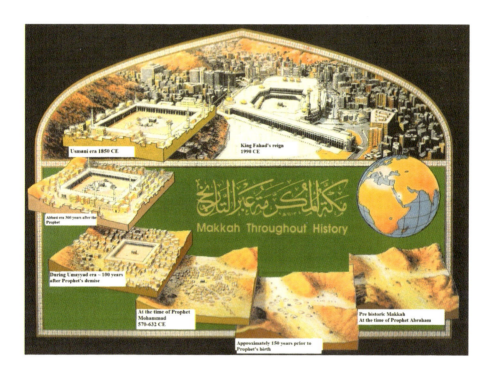

2. A Laudable Saudi Initiative for Interfaith Dialogue

I salute the visionary leadership of King Abdullah of Saudi Arabia for organizing a three day conference (June 2008) for Muslim scholars to stress the need for an interfaith dialogue. It was the hope of the organizers that the meeting would reach an agreement on a global Islamic charter on the dialogue with Christians and Jews.

In his opening speech the King elaborated on the purpose of the conference with these remarks, "We need to counter challenges of rigidity, ignorance, narrow mindedness and to make the world accommodate the concepts and the prospects of the kind message of Islam without enmity or antagonism." At a time when right wing religious extremists in both the Western and the Islamic world are fueling the concept of a "clash of civilizations," those advocating dialogue for peaceful coexistence of cultures deserve our appreciation.

During the last five decades the Roman Catholic Church has been in the forefront advocating interfaith dialogues with the explicit understanding that the new realities of our present interdependent world requires that the Christian world "maintain good fellowship among the nations...if possible to live for their part in peace with all men so that they may truly be sons [obedient] of the Father [God] who is in heaven" (Nostra Aetate [In our time] by Pope Paul VI, October 28, 1965)."

"Nostra Aetate" also expressed regard and esteem for Muslims and exonerated all Jews except those few in Jesus's time who hatched a conspiracy against him. Understanding that although in the course of centuries, many quarrels have arisen between Christians and Muslims, the synod urged all to forget the past and work together for social justice and moral welfare, as well as for peace and freedom.

More recently, Pope Benedict pleaded to the followers of Abrahamic faiths in similar terms, saying, "Judaism, Christianity and Islam believe in the one God, Creator of heaven and earth. It follows, therefore, that all three monotheistic religions are called to cooperate with one another for the common good of humanity, serving the cause of justice and peace in the world" (March 16, 2006). It is important here to ponder the term "justice" which the church is so ardently putting forward for consideration. Because Pope Benedict himself has a background in philosophy before he was ordained in the Catholic Church, it is important to understand the concept of justice from a philosopher's perspective, and here I would like to reference Socrates.

We find in Plato's work "*The Republic*" Socrates questioning Cephalus, Polemarchus, and others to elicit from them the true nature of justice. Cephalus suggested that justice means telling the truth and paying one's debts. In antithesis Socrates points out that if you borrow a weapon from a friend who then goes mad and loses his mind and demands it back, you will feel it inappropriate and unjust to hand back the weapon. According to Socrates, this insight illustrates the need to produce a new definition of justice to include both the original contention and the contrary case. Therefore, it is quite natural to assume that any sincere effort of an interfaith dialogue in today's world has to pass through certain stages in which thesis will produce an antithesis and both will resolve in a synthesis provided the participants in such dialogue are seekers of truth because we know from Jesus Christ that it is only the truth that sets anybody free. (John 3:21, 8:38)

But do we really need an interfaith dialogue in today's world, the concept of which was new, and for what reason? Why, like the Catholic Church, are many Muslim and Jewish scholars of our times advocating dialogue as a means to the peaceful resolution of conflicts?

To find the answer we need to look around the world we are living in, and we will appreciate the fact that the collective conscience of humanity has evolved to a stage where many of the injustices of the past, both social and religious, are less appealing to the intellect of the world masses. Philosophers of science describe this phenomenon as "paradigm shift," a point when new information and evolution in knowledge about a scientific subject forces scientists to give up old models and compels them to find new ones to describe how things now look.

Likewise, when applied by theologians the concept of a paradigm shift acknowledges that one's faiths can no longer be contained within old theories but rather must incorporate new insights. Faced with the new reality of our interdependent world, which many of us would like to call a global village, the need of the hour is a Copernican revolution in theologians' attitudes toward other faiths. As we know, the astronomical findings by Copernicus (1473–1543 CE) transformed the Ptolemaic map of the universe, so that people thereafter knew that the earth was not the center of the solar system, but rather it revolved around the sun with the other planets.

However, any tolerance toward other faiths has to originate within one's own religious beliefs. Just like the Roman Catholic Church, which exonerated today's Jews from charges of Christ's crucifixion, many modern Jewish scholars now regard Jesus as a revolutionary and do not use abusive language against him or his mother, quite contrary to what the rabbis of Jesus's time preached. Similarly, Muslims of today have to search the Islamic literature and see what it really teaches about different religious communities. After all, we are commanded in the Holy Quran to "Help ye one another in righteousness and piety, but help ye not one another in sin and rancor" (Holy Quran 5:3). Is it not true that during its early formative years Islam commanded Muslims to invite Jews and Christians to settle on common terms, the logical first step toward peaceful coexistence with other religions (Holy Quran 3:64). However, fourteen hundred years down the road, our task is compounded by the fact that we do not only need an ethic of agreement, but also an ethic for coping with disagreement. Fortunately, the Holy Quran does tell us that in such situations one can peacefully move forward by stating "To you be your way, and to me mine" (Holy Quran 109:6).

We know from the early history of Islam that Prophet Mohammad (PBUH) had a congenial interaction with the Christians of his time, who included Waraqah bin Nawfal, a scholar of Makkah; Bohira, a monk of Syria; and the Christians of Najran from southern Arabia. We also know that during the early days of the Prophet's ministry the Abyssinian king, Negus, granted refuge and protection to those Muslims who faced persecution in Makkah. It is not surprising to see that the Holy Quran speaks highly of Christians: "Nearest to the Muslims in love wilt thou find those who say 'We are Christians' because amongst them are men devoted to learning and men who have renounced the world, and they are not arrogant" (Holy Quran 5:85). However, when confronted with theological issues that were non-compromising in nature certain Trinitarian Christians are criticized, too, for their religious beliefs related to the Trinity (Holy Quran 5:75–76).

Quite similarly, careful reading of the Holy Quran with attention to the context in which certain verses were revealed makes it evident that it respects certain groups of Jews, and seems to think certain other groups of Jews are not observing Judaism to perfection. For example, it teaches Muslims to acknowledge all Hebrew prophets, including Noah, Abraham, Isaac, Jacob, Joseph, Moses, David, and Solomon, to name a few (may peace and blessings be upon all of them), teaching that they all were God's rightly guided who should be respected and Muslims should not prefer one over the other because all have similar stature in the sight of God (Holy Quran 2:136). The personality of patriarch Abraham is so central to Islamic faith that the Holy Quran commanded Prophet Mohammad to "Follow the religion of Abraham, a man of pure faith, who was not of the polytheists" (Holy Quran 16:120–123). Not only that, but Muslims are required in every ritual prayer to send peace and blessings to Prophet Abraham (PBUH) and his followers as they send peace and blessings to Prophet Mohammad (PBUH) and his followers.

It is interesting here to note that the Holy Quran exonerated Jews from charges of Jesus Christ's death and crucifixion stating, "They killed him not, neither crucified him but the matter was made dubious…for of a surety they killed him not…but God raised him up unto Himself" (Holy Quran 4:157). I think that was one of the reasons that throughout centuries Jews lived in relative peace and harmony in the Muslim dominated areas. In fact, early Islam was so inclusive to others that God Almighty in the Holy Quran declared, "Those who believe [in the Quran], and those who follow the Jewish [scripture], and the Christians and the Sabians; any who believe in God and the last day, and work righteousness shall have their reward with their Lord; and on them shall be no fear, nor shall they grieve" (Holy Quran 2:62). In another place, it is also said "Not all of them are alike; a party of the people of the Scripture (Jews and Christians) stands for the right; they recite the verses of God during the hours of the night and prostrate themselves in adoration. They believe in God and the last day; they enjoin what is right, and forbid what is wrong; and they hasten (in emulation) in (all) good works; they are in the ranks of the righteous. Of the good works they do, nothing will be rejected of them; for God knoweth well those that do right" (Holy Quran 3:113–115). Yet in other places, we do find words of criticism toward certain Jews who were in religious confrontation with Prophet Mohammad's preaching.

It is important to realize that Islam does not apply an "all or none" law to describe good or bad characters of a nation; therefore, Muslims should also refrain from generalization. The Holy Quran's censure of certain groups of Jews and Christians is not

something unique to Islam. As we know from religious literature, every new religion establishes its "correctness" by pointing
to the perceived wrongs in other established religions. Judaism,
according to the Hebrew Bible, did the same to the pagan
nations and even to their own fellow Jews whom they perceived
deviated from God's command; Christianity did the same to
Jews citing Jesus's criticism toward those Jews who disagreed
with his preaching.

3. Dialogue between Abrahamic faiths

I commend Pope John Paul II, whose quarter century reign clearly changed the two thousand year history of relations between the Roman Catholic Church and the Jews. I believe that if time had permitted him, he would have definitely generated a similar constructive dialogue with the Muslims as on many occasions he expressed his wish to do so.

Two important events have drawn my attention in the last few years. The first was Pope Benedict XVI's address to the leaders of the "American Jewish Committee" in the Vatican; the other was the "Second World Congress of Imams and Rabbis for Peace," in which seventy-two Muslim clerics and seventy-two rabbis took part in a three-day conference held in Spain, sponsored by a Paris-based peace foundation, Hommes de Parole.

In the footsteps of Pope John Paul II, Pope Benedict also tried to reach out to Muslims with these words, "Judaism, Christianity and Islam believe in the one God, Creator of heaven and earth. It follows, therefore, that all three monotheistic religions are called to cooperate with one another for the common good of humanity, serving the cause of justice and peace in the world" (March 16, 2006).

His words reflect his sincere intentions and it is now the duty of Muslim clerics to seriously take up this initiative and come up with a team of Muslim scholars that could be assembled under the auspices of "The Organization of Islamic Conference (OIC)" for this history-making event—possibly the first interfaith dialogue between the three different Abrahamic faiths.

In the post Holocaust era many sessions of interfaith dialogues have taken place between the Roman Catholics and the Jews, essentially focusing on the most sensitive issues affecting the Jewish people, namely, the Church's attitudes toward the common history related to Christology, its stance in respect to the mission of the Jews, and its position regarding the State of Israel. Like our Jewish brethren, I am convinced that Muslims as well as Christians can cite many genuine grievances from the past, but it is the future we all need to focus on and, as is said by the Pope, for the purpose of "serving the cause of Justice and peace in the world."

I think this noble cause in itself can serve as an agenda for a possible future dialogue between the different Abrahamic faiths. It reminds me of the Quranic command to Muslims stating, "Let not the hatred of others to you make you swerve to wrong and depart from justice. Be just: that is next to piety: and fear God. For God is well acquainted with all that ye do" (Holy Quran 5:8). The conference in Spain (March 20, 2006) was designed to let religious leaders discuss what role they can play in conflict resolution and in educating young people about religious tolerance. It was addressed by the Chief Rabbi of Israel, Yoma Metzger, and Imad al Falouji, the Imam of Gaza, besides other dignitaries. A sound suggestion from the conference that I liked the most was the proposal to form a "United Religious Body" just like the secular United Nations, for the purpose of conflict resolution in the religious sphere. Even though the world is ruled by secular forces, the conflicts we face today, especially post 9/11, have a deep religious basis for which we definitely need a forum where those differences can be debated. My humble opinion is that the best place for such an organization will be in Jerusalem, the city of peace.

4. Extremism in Abrahamic Faiths: Its Causes and Cure

Prophet Mohammad once told his companions that Muslims will follow the footsteps of Jews and Christians (their religious cousins) span by span and cubit by cubit, so much so that if they have entered a hole of a mastigure Muslims, too, will follow them there (*Sahih Bukhari*). One may appreciate the genius of the Prophet's statement as well as the prophecy hidden in his saying by identifying many similarities in the religious and political history of Judeo-Christianity and Islam. Because Islam is the youngest of the three Abrahamic faiths, identification of certain traits in its predecessor religions might help us better understand our modern day problems and their solutions.

You'll agree that Islam as a religion is far closer to the Judeo-Christian traditions than to any other religion, such as Hinduism, Buddhism, or Confucianism. Both Judaism and Islam share a belief in divine law that regulates all aspects of human activity from the cradle to the grave. All three religions have their own period of triumph in history; their belief that they alone are the chosen people of God and therefore the fortunate recipient and custodian of God's final message to humanity, which makes it their duty to bring this message to the rest of the world. This doctrine of election did not so much proclaim a privileged status (as the more easy-going often like to think, a phenomenon common to all Abrahamic faiths) as a glorious destiny and an ineluctable fate but a responsibility to fellow human beings (Holy Bible Amos 3:2). Unfortunately, corrupted "privileged" mentality and "chosen of God" ideologies prevent a rational thought process in its adherents and thus lead them to quickly resort to intolerance and violence.

It is true that all three religions had a tolerant and a humble beginning where the act of war was either deferred or refused, as was done by early Muslims of Makkah and the ancient Israelites of Sinai desert respectively. Christianity, too, grew and developed as a religion of the downtrodden with frequent references to Jesus Christ's preaching "render unto Caesar the things which belong to Caesar's; and unto God the things which are God's" (Mark 12:17).

But once weak, all three became triumphant in due course, with Jews citing King David's monarchy, Christians the conversion of Emperor Constantine and Christianization of the Roman Empire, and Muslims the establishment of Islamic statehood by Prophet Mohammad and the first four rightly guided Caliphs as the golden era and zenith of their respective faiths. Like all great civilizations these faith-based civilizations, too, suffered losses and defeats. However, the adherents of their respective faiths find consolation in striving to achieve that golden era once again. This, therefore, inspires both the revivalists as well as the extremists.

The most important period of Jewish history, which defined the fate of Jewish people for the last two millennia, started after the arrival of Alexander the Great in 330 BCE and lasted up to 135 CE when Roman Emperor Hadrian banished the Jews from Palestine and scattered them throughout the Roman Empire as a final solution for their constant rebellion and unrest. Being the "chosen people" of God, it was difficult for Jews to comprehend that God would allow the heathen Greco-Romans to enslave them and occupy their lands. As a result, many violent revolutionary groups emerged, including Maccabees, Zealots, Scarii, and others. Among them, the Maccabees were the only ones able to defeat the Greeks and establish their own rule— until the arrival of the Romans, who successfully eradicated each and every one of them. The rallying cry of these groups was "no lord but God," refuting man made Greco-Roman laws. It also provided a reason for condemning to death those of their fellow Jews who cooperated with the Romans and did not follow their brand of ideology. In addition to the violent groups there were also apocalyptic visionaries who called their followers in a divine war against Rome. They called the people to return to their true faith, not to arms, expecting God to fight for them through miracles, especially by letting the Messiah appear.

Unfortunately, it was only after the fall of Jerusalem and the total destruction of Solomon's temple at the hands of the Romans in 70 CE, that Josephus (a priest and commander of Jewish armies) realized that those few Jews who recklessly led the nation into revolt were entirely idiosyncratic. Their mad squabbling among themselves and ruthless behavior in Jerusalem proved that they were only out for personal gain. As for the Romans, Josephus inferred from their obvious supremacy that God was on their side and Jews were committing a sin fighting against them. In the course of his oration to those warring Jews, Josephus stated, "God when he had gone round the nations, bringing to each in turn the rod of empire, now rested over Italy." It is thus that he was able to say in the same context that Fortune, that unconditional, absolute, and predetermined divine favor, had passed over to the Romans (Flavius Josephus, *The War of the Jews* 5.367).

Clearly many parallels in Muslim history can be drawn from the above mentioned Jewish account. In the last two centuries Muslims, too, have lost two of their great empires, Ottoman and Mogul, to European colonialists. Because they, too, believe in the "chosen" status, many violent revolutionary groups can be cited in the last two or three centuries, especially armed with the concept of "Mehdi," a redeemer who, like the Jewish Messiah, is expected to appear before the end of time and fight on their behalf. The most recent such group was the Taliban, who in trying to fulfill the prophecy of Prophet Mohammad that "Mehdi's army will come out of Khurrasan [Afghanistan] holding black flags [a weak tradition from *Musnad Ahmad, Hakim and Ibn Majja*]," colored their turbans black for obvious political reasons. [Former Pakistani President Pervez Musharraf in his book described Talibans as having been "fired by a misplaced Messianic zeal," essentially endorsing my injunction (*In the Line of Fire; A Memoir* 202)]. Because the apocalyptic visionary groups believe in self-righteousness, they see fit to kill anybody who does not follow their ideologies. This was the case behind the murder of Egyptian President Anwar Saadat and the attempt on the life of President Pervez Musharraf, both professed Muslims.

Clearly, like Judaism before, Islam is in a state of both religious and political crisis, especially within itself. Many of its sects, because of divergent religious ideologies, consider each other apostate and therefore condemnable to death. The situation becomes more evident with the disappearance of law and order — as, for example, in Afghanistan and Iraq, where sectarian violence has killed more people than the war. Because no Muslim leader has been able to eradicate the theological differences and unite the Muslims into one body, it is in their own interests to at least provide a common enemy, which could be either communism or capitalism. Which one does not matter much, as long as this diversion serves the purpose. The situation is akin to that during Pope Urban II's reign (1095 CE), when he was unable to prevent the split in the Catholic Church on the issue of Jesus Christ's status in the trinity, resulting in the Eastern orthodox and Western churches. The pope called for crusades (holy war) to expel the infidels (Muslims) from the Holy Land as a means to divert the attention of the people from an issue that the Church was unable to settle effectively.

To make our world a safer place both the Muslims as well as the Western world have to work positively, keeping the larger good of humanity in mind. To this end, Muslim clerics and political leaders should focus inward and try to resolve the theological differences in the Islamic world, reducing the perceived need for an outward enemy and an appeal to violent groups. As for the Western powers, resolving the long-standing political conflicts in Kashmir, Chechnya, and Palestine is all that is required, as has been pleaded many times in the past by the Pakistani authorities.

5. Jews and Jerusalem in Christianity and Islam

Many in the Muslim world believe that the unconditional American support for Israel is due to the economic power of American Jews who are in control of America's political and financial institutions. This superiority is helping them acquire domination over the media, swaying American public opinion in favor of Jews in general and Israel in particular. Unfortunately, what Muslims do not realize is that Jews have a long history of persecution in the West, spanning over the last two millennia, the main cause of which was a religious charge that they participated in the crucifixion of Jesus Christ. Evolution in the religious thought process of Judeo-Christianity has led to accommodation between these two historic rival religions, and I believe that by generating a similar constructive dialogue between different Abrahamic faiths, including Islam, Christianity, and Judaism, specifically focusing on the commonalities of these religions, we can foster a peaceful and just global society.

The Jews' persecution at the hands of Christians started many centuries ago under the Roman Catholic tradition, which became the official religion of the Roman Empire when Constantine the Great converted to Christianity in 325 CE.

Though the New Testament (60–110 CE) records that both Jews and Romans acted in concert and therefore were equally responsible for crucifying Jesus, the later Jewish sages in their book of traditions — the Talmud (200 CE) — made the situation even worse by taking the sole responsibility of this alleged act upon themselves (excluding the Roman involvement), raised doubts of promiscuity about Jesus's miraculous birth, and attributed many of his miracles to magic. These Jewish charges against Jesus and his mother led to many "holocausts" (burnt offerings to God) by Christians of Europe; the last one, in Nazi Germany, resulted in the death of some six million Jews.

The Roman Catholic Church taught that Jews were not the chosen people of God anymore; rather, Christians were, and Jerusalem was no more the seat of God's glory on earth but that it had shifted to Rome instead. That is why we do not see any effort on the part of the Roman Empire and the early Catholic Church to give any leverage to Jews to establish a government of their own in Jerusalem or to rebuild Solomon's temple after its destruction by the Romans in 70 CE after a failed Jewish coup against the earlier Roman authorities. The event was seen as fulfillment of Christ's prophecy that "There will not be left here [temple] one stone upon another that shall not be thrown down" (Mark 13:2). In fact, the very site where the temple once stood was used by the Catholics for the city's dump until it was personally cleaned by Caliph Umar and the other companions of the Prophet Mohammad (peace be upon him) when the Muslim armies first conquered Jerusalem in 638 CE.

In the Christian world, Jews got a major breakthrough after the Protestant reformation movement of the sixteenth century that challenged the authority of the Roman Catholic Church. As Protestants drifted away from Rome they reinstated the central role of Jews and Jerusalem in formulating the Protestant doctrine for their fellow Christians. For Protestants, the more anti-Roman Catholic you were, the more Jew oriented you had to become.

As soon as Jesus was seen first as a Jew, the plight and suffering of Jewish people living in Europe finally became apparent to the Christians, which ultimately paved the path for accepting the Jews' right to have a country of their own as Israel (Balfour Declaration, Nov. 2, 1917). Now the natural follow-up in the present-day is a wish to rebuild Solomon's temple where Jesus Christ once preached, along with a renewed anticipation that Christ on his second coming will reappear in the new temple — an adulteration of the prophecies of the Jews, who are still waiting for their own Messiah to appear. Many of these Protestant sects follow laws and commandments of the Jewish Bible (Old Testament) and call themselves Jewish-Christians in an effort to keep their Jewish linkage alive, a sharp contrast to typical Roman Catholic teachings.

Finally, the horrible events of the Holocaust during World War II became a catalyst that triggered a desire in the Roman Catholic Church to change the anti-Jewish sentiments in its liturgy when the Holocaust unveiled to the Church the disastrous consequences of such preaching. In 1962, Pope Paul convened a Vatican Council that led to the famous declaration called "Nostra Aetate" (In our time), which stated, "Although the Church is the new people of God, the Jews should not be presented as repudiated or cursed by God, as if such views followed from the Holy Scripture" (James Carroll, *Constantine's Sword* 38).

Jews, on the other hand, have also softened their stance on the personality of Jesus Christ. Rabbi Joseph Telushkin in his book *Jewish Literacy*, writes, "Is there a Jewish consensus on how Jews are to regard Jesus? Perhaps not, but in recent decades many Jewish scholars have tended to view him as one of several first and second century Jews who claimed to be the Messiah, and who attempted to rid Judea of its Roman oppressors" (p128).

Islam tried to give a common ground to both Jews and Christians, but unfortunately, for almost fourteen hundred years now its message has been largely misunderstood in the Judeo-Christian world. First, it acknowledged all the Hebrew prophets, including Noah, Abraham, Isaac, Jacob, Joseph, Moses, David, and Solomon — to name a few (may peace and blessings be upon all of them) — teaching that they all were God's rightly guided who should be respected and Muslims should not prefer one over the other because all have similar stature in the sight of God (Holy Quran 2:136). It also requires that in every ritual prayer Muslims should send peace and blessings to Patriarch Abraham (PBUH) and his followers as they send peace and blessings to Prophet Mohammad (PBUH) and his followers.

Second, it accepted Jesus as the awaited Messiah (Christ) who was born miraculously to pious Mary and who showed many miracles at God's will, including raising the dead and healing both those who were born blind and lepers (Holy Quran, 3:49).

Third, it exonerated Jews from charges of Christ's death and crucifixion, stating "They killed him not, neither crucified him but the matter was made dubious…. for of a surety they killed him not…but God raised him up unto Himself" (Holy Quran, 4:157). Maybe that was one of the reasons Jews lived in relative peace and harmony in the Muslim dominated areas.

Fourth, it taught that the Temple mount in Jerusalem is a holy place that is one of the oldest places for worship on earth. In the Arabic traditions it is called "Masjid Al-Aqsa," meaning the farthest mosque (Holy Quran 17:1). The mosque is considered the third holiest site in Islam after Kabah in Makkah and the Mosque of the Prophet Mohammad in Medina. In fact, the mosque is considered as old as Kabah itself, with a difference of mere forty years between their constructions (*Sahih Bukhari*). A reference to this ancient site can also be found in the Bible, which tells that "the King priest of Salam (Jerusalem) paid homage to Prophet Abraham who in return gave tithe to the priest" (Gen. 14:18), implying its existence well before Prophet Abraham's time.

Israelites took hold in this area after King David's conquest in the land and his son Solomon is said to have built the famous Solomon's temple in the tenth century BCE. The temple was laid to ruins by the Babylonians in 586 BCE. They were later defeated by the Persians, who allowed the reconstruction of the temple in 520 BCE. An enormous building project at the temple site was carried out by King Herod, who reigned in Palestine from 37 to 4 BCE, and the temple was finally destroyed by the Roman legions in 70 CE.

The original Solomon's temple was basically rectangular in shape, about 105 feet long, 35 feet wide and 52 feet high. The innermost chamber in the temple was called the "holy of holies" and, like the Kabah of Makkah, was a cube with a door. It measured 10x10x10 meters and housed the "Ark of the covenant." The floor of the "holy of holies" was slightly elevated, and if that was the very site of the "foundation stone" (Eben Shetiyyah) or "the rock" of Jewish traditions upon which the world was founded is a matter of scholarly debate. Like the Muslims, the Israelites did not believe that God's presence could be localized or confined to a particular building, but the Temple did symbolize a divine dwelling place and assured the people of ready access to their God.

"Solomon's Temple (Hakal-e-Sulaymani)"

Because Jews in ancient times faced the "holy of holies" for their prayers and sacrifices, early Muslims who evolved from the old "Abrahamic faith" of Arabia also faced toward Jerusalem for their ritual prayers. But as Islam slowly grew into a system of its own, the direction of Muslim prayers (Qibla) was later changed to Kabah in Makkah instead.

That was precisely the reason Caliph Umar, despite identifying "the rock" (*Sakhra* in Arabic) upon his arrival at the temple mount in 638 CE, neither prayed facing it nor built any structure upon it, because the significance of that particular spot on the temple mount was over in Islamic jurisprudence after the change of "Qibla" event in Islamic ideology. However, because of the holiness of Temple mount itself, Caliph Umar did make a small mosque in the southern corner of its platform, initially called the "mosque of Umar" and today known as "Masjid Al-Aqsa," taking caution to avoid "the rock" coming between the mosque and the direction of Kabah so that Muslims would face only Makkah when they prayed (*The History of Al-Tabri*). In fact, there is evidence to believe that early Muslims did allow Jews to pray at their own Qibla ("the rock") site just as the Christian delegation from Najran had been allowed by Prophet Mohammad (PBUH) to pray in his Medina mosque (Robert G. Hoyland, *Seeing Islam As Others Saw It* 127).

What motivated the later Umayyad Caliphs Abdul Malik Bin Marvan and his successor Walid to build the "Dome of the rock" (688–691 CE, *Quba Assakhra* in Arabic) is a topic that has baffled scholars throughout the ages and is worth searching. Many suggestions have been put forward by the scholars, such as a desire "to build a place to commemorate the heavenly journey of Prophet Mohammad," "to build a shelter for the pilgrims who came to visit the rock," "to build another Kabah like religious structure in Jerusalem," or "to make an Islamic monument larger in grandeur than the Christian monuments of the city" (Karen Armstrong, *Jerusalem* 217–244 and Said Nuseibeh and Oleg Grabar, *The Dome of The Rock* 139). Whatever might have been the intention of the Caliphs, unfortunately the Dome sent a political message to the Jews that the sons of Ishmael had established themselves at their sacred site, which triggered a strong Jewish opposition: first against the Umayyad dynasty and then the later Muslim rulers. The rift has continued to the present day (Neil Asher Silberman, *Heavenly Powers* 30).

From the preceding discussion it must be clear to my readers that all three Abrahamic faiths—Islam, Christianity, and Judaism—have much in common, and many of the differences they have can be resolved by initiating a dialogue specifically focusing on the commonalities of these religions— clearly the need of our present times.

6. Jerusalem and the True Legacy of Caliph Umar (RA)

I agree with former President Musharraf's analysis that the current wave of Muslim extremism can be severely curtailed by resolving the long-standing political conflicts in Palestine as well as in Kashmir. His opinion found strong support at the summit of the "Organization of Islamic Conference" (OIC) held in Makkah in December 2005: in the summit declaration his concern was repeated verbatim along with a renewed demand that "Jerusalem's Islamic and historic identity be preserved." I cannot say how significant the Kashmiri issue might be for the rest of the world, but for Muslims on one side and the Judeo-Christian world on the other it is the ownership and inheritance of Jerusalem, especially the temple mount, that has to be addressed before one can contemplate the prospects of peace in the region as well as in the world.

Unfortunately, the Makkah declaration has not stressed anything new on this issue; rather, it was a call to keep the status quo, which in my opinion is the main cause of delay in a meaningful Israeli-Palestinian engagement and a final step toward a free state of Palestine. Keeping the religious emotions aside, I suggest all parties critically look into their claim on the temple mount and see if they can accommodate each other.

It is the teaching of all three Abrahamic faiths—Islam, Christianity, and Judaism—that humans by design are preservers of God's doing in the world and not destroyers. The Holy Bible puts this belief beautifully by saying "God created man in his image" (Gen. 1:27), a metaphoric likeness with God the Creator and the Preserver. In the Holy Quran, God rebuked the Angels in a discourse when they argued, "Man will cause mischief in the world and shed blood" by saying, "You do not know what I know" (Holy Quran 2:30). If we are the chosen people of God, as we all claim we are, then we need to do such preserving acts as will make us worthy of God's trust, and there is no better place to start than in Jerusalem itself. Historically speaking, Jeru-salem or Uru-salem is a Babylonian name that means "city of peace." It is interesting to note that the root word "salam" means peace in other Semitic languages, including Hebrew (Shalom) and Arabic, and hence the Arabic word "Islam."

Muslims first entered Jerusalem in 638 CE and since then, more or less, they have been in control of temple mount and its platform, except for a brief period of seventy years when crusaders became victorious in the land; therefore, the covered structures one sees at the temple mount bear the signatures of Muslim architects. The two readily visible structures are the "Dome of the Rock," located in the middle and northern part of the platform, and "Al-Aqsa mosque," located at its southern corner. Other than these two, for which we have strong historic evidence of how and when they were constructed, there are many small monuments located at the platform "mythically" attributed to Hebrew prophets and Prophet Mohammad's heavenly journey. The doubts about their authenticity are strengthened by the fact that Prophet Mohammad (PBUH) on this heavenly journey arrived in Jerusalem alone and Muslims only entered Jerusalem five years after his demise.

The famous ninth century Muslim historian Al-Tabri is an important read on the topic of Muslim conquest in the region of Syria-Palestine. It was interesting to find that Caliph Umar

(RA), who was busy in a military campaign at a Syrian front, advanced his armies in Jerusalem only at the request and instigation of a Jew.

Al-Tabri tells the story that when Caliph Umar arrived at the temple mount he summoned Ka'ab Ahbar, a prominent Jewish convert to Islam, to help identify "Sakhra" (the "rock" or the "foundation stone") of Jewish traditions, upon which the world was founded. For Caliph Umar, this spot signified the first Qibla, the direction of Muslim prayers, which Prophet Mohammad used until 622 CE, when it was changed to Kabah in Makkah for eternity (Holy Quran 2:142–145). After the identification of "Sakhra," he then asked Ka'ab where in his opinion Muslims should put their Qibla (meaning toward "Sakhra" or the "Kabah"), to which Ka'ab replied, "Toward Sakhra." Caliph Umar, showing his resentment of this opinion, said, "We Muslims are commanded to face Kabah." Having said that, he faced Makkah in the southern corner of the platform to offer his prayers, where later the mosque was constructed that today is called Masjid Al-Aqsa.

One wonders why Caliph Umar asked a question to which he already knew the answer and especially to a former Jew and not the other senior companions of Prophet Mohammad (PBUH) who were also present at the occasion. Clearly, what Caliph Umar and the other companions have shown here is a unanimous reaffirmation that as Kabah had become the center of their prayers by a divine decree, the significance of "Sakhra" in Islamic jurisprudence was over and they had nothing to do with it anymore.

We also read that during the same time period Caliph Umar, accompanied with Sophronius, the patriarch of Jerusalem, paid a visit to the Church of the Holy Sepulcher (the site of Jesus Christ's alleged resurrection from death), the most important Christian monument of Jerusalem. As the time for afternoon prayer approached, Sophronius invited Caliph Umar to pray inside the church. Caliph Umar declined his invitation and prayed outside, citing his fear that Muslims who would come after him might establish a mosque in place of the church if he would pray over there. And this is exactly what had happened over the years — a mosque bearing the name of Caliph Umar was constructed next to the Church of Holy Sepulcher that is present to this day.

If not a metaphor, these historic accounts are clear evidence that early Muslims were very conscious of what belonged to them and what belonged to the others, the distinction of which unfortunately became blurred after the construction of the "Dome of the Rock" in 691 CE by Ummayad Caliphs Abdul Malik Bin Marvan and his son Walid, some fifty years after the time of many righteous Caliphs.

Islamic civilization was established on the principles of justice not only for the Muslims but for other religious communities, too. It is an injustice to the Jews that they are not allowed to visit the "rock," which to them carries the same religious importance as Muslims have for Kabah. I think thirty-five acres of platform at the temple mount is not a small land, and dividing it between Muslims and Jews will herald a new era of understanding and cooperation between the two.

7. The Bible and the Quran

I n "The Bible and the Quran" (*Newsweek,* February 11, 2002), Mr. Kenneth L. Woodward discusses a topic very relevant to the current political situation. He tries to probe the conflict line between Islamic and Western Judeo-Christian civilizations, but fails to elaborate the Quranic point of view with accuracy, thus leaving readers to rely heavily on assumptions. Although most of the objectionable statements were addressed by the letters published in PakistanLink.com, yet a few questions raised by the author still remain to be addressed.

Question: "Is Islam an inherently intolerant faith?" "Does the Quran oblige Muslims to wage jihad — Holy war — on those who do not share their belief?"

The answer to these two questions is a simple *no,* as the Quran explicitly commands its adherents: "There is no compulsion in religion" (Holy Quran 2:256). The life and property of all the citizens living in an Islamic state are considered sacred whether a person is Muslim or not. The only religion on earth that teaches this magnitude of tolerance is Islam; you will not find any other religion in the world with such a bold written expression.

Question: "Who are these 'infidels' that the Muslim scriptures find so odious? After all, Jews and Christians are monotheists, too…" (Insinuating that infidels and Jews/ Christians are considered the same in the Quran).

Answer: "Infidels" are the non-believers in any kind of divine revelation. In the Quran, Jews and Christians are called "People of the Book" (possessors of divine revelations), as the author himself acknowledges, and they should not be lumped together with infidels.

Question: "Listening to the rant of Osama Bin Laden and other radical Islamists, Jews and Christians wonder who really speaks for Islam in these perilous times."

Answer: Every religion on earth is known to have extremists, but it is my humble opinion that the ideology of a few should not be the reason for putting a religion on trial. Has anyone ever raised a finger to Christianity on the basis of what Timothy McVeigh did in Oklahoma City? Obviously not, and on the same basis we should stop judging Islam wrongly.

Question: "What common ground—if any—joins these three 'People of the Book,' as Muslims call their fellow monotheists?"

Question: "What seeds of reconciliation lie within the Quran and the Bible and the traditions that they represent?"

Answer: First we need to remember the Shem (Kalima) of Bani Israel when Moses at Sinai said, "Shama Yezrael Adonai Elohayno Adonai Ekhad" (Hear O' Israel, The Lord is our God, The Lord is one (Deut. 6:4). This same message was repeated word by word by Jesus Christ (the Messiah) when the Jews asked him the first commandment and he replied, "Hear O' Israel, The Lord is our lord God, The Lord is one" (Mark12: 28–29). And finally, in the Quran this eternal message was repeated through Prophet Mohammad (PBUH), "And your God is one God: There is no god but He, Most Gracious, Most Merciful" (Holy Quran 2:163). It does not require a rocket scientist to appreciate the commonality between these religions.

Surprisingly, the common ground that joins these monotheistic religions was elaborated in the Quran some fourteen hundred years ago in a very peaceful and tolerant way. "You Say: O People of the Book, Come to common term between us and you: that we shall worship none but God, and that we shall ascribe no partners unto Him, and that none of us shall take others for lords beside God. And if they turn away, then say: Bear witness that we are they who have surrendered (unto Him)" (3:64).

Question: "Does the battle of the books that has endured for centuries between Muslims and the believers in the west ensure a perpetual "Clash of Civilizations"?

Answer: The famous scholar Mr. Samuel Huntington, who initially proposed this theory, in his article in the Newsweek special edition (December 2001), refuted the idea that the conflict in Afghanistan is a manifestation of the "Clash of Civilizations." Let's hope he is right in his assessment, as the world is desperate to see an end to this ongoing conflict.

8. Eid-ul-Adha: The Moral Lesson

Each and every year Muslims all over the world celebrate Eid-Ul-Adha, a day to commemorate the sacrificial act of Prophet Abraham (PBUH). Both the Judeo-Christian and the Islamic traditions affirm that Prophet Abraham was tested by God Almighty in the one thing he held most dear to his heart: a vision wherein he was to sacrifice his only son to God. When Abraham discussed his vision with his son (Ishmael) (PBUH), Ishmael replied, "O my father do as you are commanded. You shall, by God's will, find me to be among the patient."

Abraham took his son Ishmael and placed him on the ground and when he was about to sacrifice Ishmael, God called out "O Abraham! Thou hast already fulfilled the vision! This was indeed a manifest trial." God then provided him a ram to sacrifice in place of his son and a reward for his sincere intentions. Afterward, God blessed Abraham with a second son, Isaac (PBUH), a great and righteous prophet. The story can be found in the pages of the Holy Quran Chapter 37, verses 100–113.

The biblical story in the book of Genesis differs by naming Isaac as the favorite son, stating, "And God said, take now thy son, thine only son Isaac, whom thou lovest, and get thee into the land of Moriah; and offer him there for a burnt offering upon one of the mountains which I will tell thee of" (Gen. 22:2). Other than that difference, the stories in the Holy Quran and the Bible are in agreement that God did not want Abraham to actually sacrifice his son, but the purpose of this trial was to test his loyalty. Here, too, God stops Abraham at the last minute and makes Isaac's sacrifice unnecessary by providing a ram, caught in some nearby bushes, to be sacrificed instead.

Though the Holy Quran (Chapter 37) does not spell out the name of Ishmael in the text (Arabic), in the Muslim mind the likelihood of him being the sacrificial one is strengthened by the fact that the Quran immediately after mentioning the story of sacrifice (37:99–111) says, "And We gave him (Abraham) the glad tidings of Isaac, a prophet, one of the righteous" (112–113). One who was not born yet (Isaac) cannot be the sacrificial one. Similarly the "only son" of Bible cannot be Isaac, because even the Bible is in agreement that Isaac was Abraham's second son, and at a time when Abraham had only "one son," it was Ishmael.

The famous thirteenth century Muslim scholar Ibn Kathir in his renowned book *Stories of the Prophets* is of the opinion that the biblical account of naming Isaac was tampered with at the hands of some Jewish scribes. He further elaborates his point by saying,

> The only thing which could have incited them to tamper with this is their jealousy with Arabs. Ishmael is the father of Arabs who lived in the area of Hijaz, from which our Prophet (Mohammad) (PBUH) came. Isaac is the father of Jacob, who was called Israel, to whom they relate to. They wanted to take away this honor from Arabs, and so they tempered with the Book of God with omissions and additions. (153)

Regardless of whether the sacrificial one was Ishmael or Isaac, I believe both the sons of Abraham were righteous prophets and if asked, would have shown the same obedience to their father in fulfilling his vision without asking a single question. Even if we agree for the sake of discussion that there truly was a rivalry between Bani Ishmael and Bani Isaac as Ibn Kathir suggested, the message of monotheism that came out of Abraham's family deserves more discussion than the political feud within the family, which serves nothing, but smears the characters of these mighty prophets and sows hatred among the followers of Abrahamic faiths to no avail.

In such debates we often overlook the fact that killing of human beings, especially children, was a common religious practice in ancient cultures. It was common among agrarian societies, e.g. in the ancient Middle East, where the sacrifice of humans to pagan gods was a normal way of showing one's devotion and loyalty to the deity, guaranteeing the fertility of their soils. In ancient China and Egypt, human sacrifice was connected with ancestor worship in which slaves and servants were killed or buried alive along with the deceased kings in order to provide service in the afterlife. The practice was widely prevalent even across the Atlantic, and there is archeological evidence that the South American Aztecs sacrificed annually to the sun, and the Incas made human sacrifice on the accession of their rulers.

It is immaterial to me which son of Abraham fulfilled his vision because I read the story of sacrifice in the context of ancient Middle Eastern cultures, which in those days favored human sacrifice. I am in favor of the modern understanding of the text, where God inspired Abraham in order to teach him a lesson that human sacrifice is abhorrent and it is the surrender of one's will alone that God required. I believe all civilizations of the world are indebted to Abraham's family, who demonstrated the moral lesson of their sacrificial act in such a way that abolished the era of human sacrifice in favor of animal sacrifice.

9. Grave and Ancestor Worship in Abrahamic Faiths

(Original article co-authored with Dr. Naseemuddin Khurram)

During his life, Prophet Mohammad (PBUH) denounced every form of Shirk, the act of associating anything or anybody with God Almighty in His attributes and powers, a sin considered unforgivable in Islamic theology (Quran 4:116) if not repented during the sinner's earthly life. Because ancestor worship and one's association with their graves was a common religious practice in pre-Islamic Arabia, Prophet Mohammad, even on his deathbed, warned Muslims not to imitate Jews and Christians who earlier had venerated the graves of their prophets and saints (Sahih Muslim, Mishkat).

But before we proceed with our inquiry into this important topic, let us first review a few terms, especially in the context of ancient cultures. By definition ancestor worship is the adoration or payment of homage to a deceased parent or ancestor. In this type of worship, usually reserved for deities, a devotee claimed spiritual relationship to the deceased. One can easily find several examples of deification of ancestors in Indian,

Mesopotamian, and Egyptian mythologies. In such cultures it is quite conceivable that even a "living" ruler could easily proclaim divinity without much problem, as was done by the Pharaoh saying to Moses and his own courtiers, "I am your God, Most High" (Quran 79:24)

Grave worship, much like ancestor worship, involves adoration of the deceased with a belief that certain departed spirits must be fed or honored. With this, they could become channels of information with the spiritual world (necromancy) and intercessors with God Almighty. Excessive reverence and love for the deceased and a belief in afterlife in the worldly grave was apparently the reason behind such practices. It is important to realize that throughout human history idols were actually made in remembrance of those departed "saintly" souls. To make us understand the Quranic verse in which the adversaries of Prophet Noah said to their fellow compatriots, "(you) must not forsake Wadd, Suwaa, Yaghuth, Yauq and Nasr" (71:23), Abdullah Bin Abbas (RA) explained that they were the saintly men who followed Noah's monotheistic religion and when they died, people associated themselves with their dead cult, made idols in their resemblance, and started worshipping them (*Sahih Bukhari*; Commentary of Chapter Noah from the Holy Quran).

According to the Bible, Israelites, too, were forbidden to practice dead worship, but they often departed from God's injunctions and participated in such practices (1 Sam. 28:1). They were specifically warned neither to offer to the dead (Deut. 26:14) nor to consult the dead in an effort to learn the future (Isa. 8:19; Isa. 65:4). Such acts were considered grave sins by the prophets and a rebellion from God's will and were strongly forbidden (Deut. 18:9–14). Despite these clear warnings, the Jewish book of traditions, the Talmud (200–600 CE), records numerous instances where people visited the graves and even spoke with the dead persons (Abraham Cohen, *Everyman's Talmud: The Major Teachings of the Rabbinic Sages*).

Today, even though learned Jews condemn such practices, popular culture knows no bounds. Recently we read an interesting news article that "hundreds of young Israeli women in a hope to find themselves a husband have been placing their underwear on the tomb of a venerated rabbi hoping that their marriage prayers will be answered" (BBC, AFP; Dec 23, 2005) http://iafrica.com/loveandsex/news/721044.htm. Though the chief rabbinate of Israel has condemned these acts as "a profanity" and "unforgivable in the sight of God," the practice still prevails.

Christians are no exception, and among them many sects are known for such practices. The Roman Catholics advocated worship of St. Peter's grave during the Easter rites. It is documented that their religious practices of worshipping the graves of the saints was a norm in ancient times, fervently done even well before the time of Prophet Mohammad himself [Monk John Moschus (550–619 CE), *The Spiritual Meadow (Pratum Spirituale)*]. More recently, the "*Catechism of the Catholic Church* (956)," under the title "The intercession of the saints," reads that the dead saints in heavens "do not cease to intercede with the Father (God) for us, as they proffer the merits which they acquired on earth through the one mediator between God and men, Christ Jesus." It further quotes a dying St. Dominic saying to his brethren, "Do not weep, for I shall be more useful to you after my death and I shall help you then more effectively than during my life" (271).

Unfortunately, despite clear instructions from Prophet Mohammad (PBUH) that "every grave should be leveled with the ground," (*Sahih Muslim*) the Prophet's fear has come true and Muslims, too, in imitation of their religious cousins the Jews and Christians, have constructed places of worship (mosques) over almost all of the graves related to the Prophets. The tombs of Prophet Abraham and Sarah in Jerusalem; Ezekiel in Keffil, Iraq; Ezra in Basra, Iraq; and Daniel in Susa, Iran, are a few examples venerated both by Jews and Muslims alike. Not only that, but Muslims have turned the grave of Prophet Mohammad and many other Muslim saints into places of worship.

The Prophet's wife Ayesha (may God be pleased with her) reported that Prophet Mohammad was buried in his house in order to prevent the possibility of his grave being worshipped (*Sahih Bukhari*). Today, with the expansion of the Prophet's mosque in Madina, Prophet Mohammad's burial ground (the house of Ayesha (RA)) is included in one of its southern corners, but the "learned" clerics do not consider it a part of the mosque—an example of self-deception indeed. The green Dome, which was originally blue in color and marked the grave of Prophet Mohammad, was constructed late in Muslim history (678 AH/1279 CE) by an Egyptian ruler, Mansoor bin Qalawoon Al-Salahi. The scholars of his times strongly opposed construction of that "dome" (Qubba) as an innovation to no avail (Samhodi, *Wafa-al-Wafa*, Vol 1:435–436).

It is important to note that Islam has allowed a Muslim to visit the graves for the very reason that it "diminishes one's inclination towards this world and reminds [one of] the realities of death and afterlife" (*Ibn Majja* and *Sahih Muslim*). For this purpose, no distinction can be made between the grave of a Muslim or a non-Muslim. It is reported that the Prophet himself had visited his mother's grave (*Sahih Muslim*). Imam Nisai, the compiler of *Sunnan Nisai,* titled one of the chapters of his book on funeral prayers "Ziyyara al-Qabar al-Mushrik" (visit to the grave of a pagan) and reported the above mentioned event of the Prophet's visit to his mother's grave in the chapter.

Unfortunately, the general Muslim perception is that only the graves of Muslims can be visited and therefore like our religious cousins—Jews and Christians—they started worshipping their respective prophets and saints. It is even said that Prophet Mohammad is alive in his "worldly" grave (God forbid) and can listen and shake hands with the visitors, despite the clear statement from the Prophet himself that after death he will be at "Al-Waseelah" the highest place in Paradise (*Sahih Bukhari*).

In the following few paragraphs we shall discuss the reliability and authenticity of narrations (hadith) presented by those who believe in the concept of life after death in the worldly grave.

1- It is reported that the Prophet said

"In your days Friday is the best of the days as Adam was created on that day and died on the same day. And on this day will be 'Blowing' (of Trumpet) and 'Lightning'; So on this day increase your blessing prayers for me (Salat-alan-Nabi) because your prayers are presented (offered) to me." The Companions said: "O Prophet how is it possible when you are dust [i.e. your body consumed by the earth upon your demise]" and the Prophet replied, "God has forbidden the earth to consume the bodies of the prophets. (*Musnad Ahmed*)

Imam Bukhari has criticized this hadith (tradition) because of a fault in the chain of narrators. According to him, first, the hadith is narrated by an unreliable narrator—Adur-Rehaman bin Yazid bin Tammem—and second, another narrator—Hussain bin Ali al-Jaffai—has intentionally changed the liar's name to Abdur-Rehman bin Yazid bin Jabbir. (Bukhari, *Tarikh al-Kabber*)

Imam Abi-Hatim al-Razi has also rejected this narration (*Illal-al-Hadith*).

Furthermore, in another tradition the Prophet had said that "every son of Adam is eaten up by dust" (Kullu Ibnu Adam yakkuluhu turab). Here no exception is mentioned for Prophets, saints, or ordinary human beings.

On the other hand, the Quran says that all deeds and matters are reported back to God (for decisions) (Holy Quran 3:109). Therefore, it should be clear that the prayer for the blessings of the Prophet, as well as all human acts and prayers go back to God Almighty alone, the disposer of all affairs.

2- To further support the cultic practices of dead worship, it is said that martyrs of Battle of Badr and Uhud are alive in their graves; but this is not correct either. The Quran says that those martyrs are "nearer to God and getting their sustenance" (Holy Quran 2:154 and 3:169).

The Prophet further explained that the martyrs' souls are in the bodies of birds residing in Paradise and their nests are hanging by the Holy Throne. The martyrs move in the Paradise as they like and then return to their dwellings. When the martyrs found such an honor they asked God Almighty that their souls be returned to their bodies (so that once more they can die in God's cause and inform their companions of such a great reward) (*Sahih Muslim*, Kitab-al-Imara). But as is ordained by God Almighty that man will have only "one earthly life" (explained below), their request was not granted, but through revelation to the Prophet it was told that they are in the best of abodes.

The Holy Quran says that there is a "Burzakh" (barrier, partition) between the departed soul and the world. By definition, Burzakh is a hindrance that could not be crossed over. As is explained in Surah Mominnon (believers), when the souls ask God Almighty to be returned to the world in order to perform the good deeds again, their request is rejected in these words: "before them (dead people) is a Burzakh till the day they are raised again" (Holy Quran 23:100).

Imam Muslim has further clarified that after death the soul is taken by the angels, and they go all the way up to the heavens until they reach the Divine presence. There it is commanded by God Almighty that the soul be kept in place until the day of resurrection (*Sahih Muslim*, No. 5119, Kitab-al-Janna wa Siffat).

3- Contrary to the above mentioned facts, the vast majority of Muslims believe that after death the soul of the deceased person is again reunited with his dead body in his worldly grave. In support of this belief a weak narration (reported by Barra bin Azzib) is presented claiming that the soul of the dead person, whether righteous or evil, returns to the body in the worldly grave, where it experiences the pleasure of heavens or torments of hell depending on its deeds. This lengthy narration is reported in *Musnad Ahmed* and *Abu Dawood*, et al.

First of all, the narration is in complete contradiction to Quranic teachings, which say that there are only two lives and two deaths for each human being (Holy Quran 2:28). The Holy Quran says that on the Day of Judgment the people will exclaim, "O God, you have given us two lives and two deaths" (Qallo Rabbana Amittana Ithnatain wa Ahyyaittana Ithnatain) (Holy Quran 40:11). This makes the matter very clear for us that for each living soul we have:

one death (era of non-existence)
one life (this worldly life)
second death (the death upon termination of this worldly life)
second life (yet to come on the day of resurrection)

Therefore it is not possible for a dead body to receive its soul back and become alive in this "worldly" grave again.

Second, the narration of Barra bin Azzib is reported by untrustworthy narrators. Third, it is the rule of hadith scholarship that if a narrator reports something in support of his cultic ideas, such report should be rejected (*Nakhbbatul-Fikar*).

The hadith under scrutiny is reported by the Shiite narrators who held the cultic views of grave worshipping. The narrators of this report are Minhal bin Umr and Zazzan; both are stalwart Shiites per Ibn Hajar and Jozzjani.

Although some Sunni scholars like Ibn-Qayyam have accepted this hadith as an authentic one, and therefore a source of inspiration to many Sunni sects believing in life after death in a worldly grave, for others the jury is still out. The report further claimed that after the soul is questioned on the seventh heaven, God commands that "soul be returned to body as it is created from dust." This idea of the soul being created from dust cannot be found in any other tradition and is in direct contradiction with the hadith of Sahih Muslim, which states that soul is kept in "place" until the day of resurrection (discussed above).

It follows, therefore, that the idea of a "third" life in the worldly grave is neither found in the Quran nor is supported by any authentic hadith from Prophet Mohammad and therefore should be questioned. Those in favor of this preconceived idea draw erroneous conclusion from the following report in Sahih Bukhari, which states that

> After the battle of Badr the prophet commanded that the dead bodies of the pagans which were laying in the battle field be thrown into a well (for mass burial). He then stayed in the battle field and on the third day went up to the well with his companions and with a loud

voice called upon the names of the famous personalities of Qurayshi pagans and asked 'Have you not found the promise of God; A truth?' (*Sahih Bukhari*)

It is argued that the dead people become alive to hear what the Prophet had to say and that this proves their point of view. In fact, the matter was made clear by another authentic hadith reported in *Sahih Bukhari* and *Sahih Muslim* where Ayesha (the Prophet's wife) said that this illustrates the fact that those pagans by then had known the truth (of Islam) and then she quoted the verse from the Holy Quran in which it is said that dead cannot be made to listen (27:80) and those who are dead and those who are living are not the same.

On the other hand, Abdullah bin Umar looked upon this event as a miracle of Prophet Mohammad where dead pagans were made to hear on that particular day. A miracle by definition is something unusual that happens in extraordinary circumstances (*Sahih al-Bukhari*).

Finally, in the Holy Quran, in a number of places, Prophet Abraham had spoken to idols, saying "why are you not eating?" Of course, he did not hold the belief that idols can listen; this is just an example of a figurative speech. This is exactly what Prophet Mohammad had shown in the battle field of Badr.

4- In another weak narration it is told that the Prophet's soul is "returned" to his body whenever someone says Salam (peace) upon him (reported in *Masnad Ahmed*).

This is, of course, quite strange. Are we to believe that multiple times the soul is given and taken out of Prophet's body, as millions of Muslims send peace blessings to him each day? The use of the word "return" is quite disturbing here, as there is no explanation justifying its use. A number of scholars have rejected this report, and many others have accepted it with no sound reasoning.

Here it is necessary to understand the phenomenon of sleep and death as is explained in the Holy Quran.

In Chapter Anam (Cattle) the Holy Quran says:

"It is He Who doth take your souls by night and hath knowledge of all that ye have done by day. By day doth He raise you up again; that a term appointed be fulfilled; in the end unto Him will be your return, then will He show you the truth of all that ye did" (Holy Quran 6:60–61).

Then in Chapter Zumur (Troops) it says:

"It is Allah that takes the souls (of men) at death: and those that die not (He takes) during their sleep: those on whom He has passed the decree of death: He keeps back (from returning to life) but the rest He sends (to their bodies) for a term appointed. Verily in this are Signs for those who reflect" (39:42).

In these verses a clear analogy between sleep and death can be appreciated except the fact that upon one's death the soul is "kept back" from returning to the earthly body until the day of resurrection.

Precisely for these reasons, upon the demise of Prophet Mohammad a consensus was reached between the Companions of the Prophet that he in fact had passed away. The final words of the first Caliph, Abu Bakar Siddiq are on record that "Whoever worshiped Mohammad must know that he is dead" (mun kanna ubbudu mohammad fa inn-na mohammadan qad maat) and the matter was concluded on that same day.

We know that the Prophet died on Monday and was buried on Tuesday. Clearly many among the Companions must have sent prayers of blessing to the Prophet after his demise but none witnessed or reported the phenomenon of his soul returning to his body. It was years later that such falsehood was concocted in his name.

We also know that the prophet has commanded Muslims to pray for him that he gets the best dwelling place, called "Al-Waseela," in Heaven, which will be given to only one person, and he wished it for himself. (*Sahih Muslim*, Kitab al-Salat, No. 577)

The Prophet himself said that he had been shown a cloud-like dwelling in the heaven, where he will come after his death. (*Sahih Bukhari*, Kitab al-Jannaiz, No. 1297)

In the presence of these reports it is clear that the Prophet is in his dwelling in the heaven. The Prophet opted to go into the divine presence instead of staying here on this earth, as at the time of his demise his last words were "Allahuma Rafiqul Aala" (O God, you are the best of Companions).

Grave and ancestor worship is strictly forbidden in all three monotheistic religions—Islam, Christianity, and Judaism. Though the prophets fought against such ideas, time and again pagan influences have corrupted the true monotheism of Abrahamic faiths.

10. Jesus Christ and Mary in Islam

I would like to start by wishing my Christian friends a very wonderful Christmas every year. Even though within Christian scholarship there is an unsettled debate of exactly when Jesus Christ was born and, therefore, his nativity; and Muslims, too, may have their own reservations, as I'll explain later, for me the importance of Christmas lies in Christ's monotheistic message: "Hear O Israel, the Lord is our God the lord is one." This message not only resonates in Christian writings, but also in the Muslim book of authority, the Holy Quran, which not many of our Christian friends are aware of and therefore requires us to share our faith.

A Muslim can rightfully boast that Islam is the only religion other than Christianity that requires its followers to believe in Jesus Christ. No Muslim can claim to be a Muslim without acknowledging Jesus Christ and his pious mother, Mary. Jesus's name is mentioned no fewer than twenty-five times in the Holy Quran and a whole chapter — Chapter Mary — is named for his mother, Mary.

The Holy Quran says,

> God did choose Adam and Noah the family of Abraham and the family of Imran above all people. Offspring one of the other; and God heareth and knoweth all things. Behold!

a woman of Imran said: "O my Lord! I do dedicate unto thee what is in my womb for thy special service so accept this of me for thou hearest and knowest all things." When she was delivered she said: "O my Lord! behold! I am delivered of a female child!" And God knew best what she brought forth, "and nowise is the male like the female. I have named her Mary and I commend her and her offspring to thy protection from the Evil one the rejected." Right graciously did her Lord accept her: He made her grow in purity and beauty; to the care of Zakariya was she assigned. Every time that he entered (her) chamber to see her he found her supplied with sustenance. He said: "O Mary! whence (comes) this to you?" She said: "From God: for God provides sustenance to whom He pleases without measure." (Holy Quran 3:33–36)

It is believed by Muslims that the house of Imran was descended from the progeny of Prophet David. Zakariya was the Prophet of that time and he was Mary's maternal relative, and as it was common among the Israelites to consecrate some of their children to the services of Solomon's temple (Hakal-e-Sulaymani), God's choice of Zakariya to be responsible for Mary's upbringing makes perfect sense. The trial Mary was destined to go through and the responsibility she was about to carry was not an ordinary one.

God further says about Mary in Chapter Al-Imran,

Behold! the angels said: "O Mary! God hath chosen thee and purified thee; chosen thee above the women of all nations. "O Mary! worship thy Lord devoutly; prostrate thyself and bow down (in prayer) with those who bow down." This is part of the tidings of the things unseen which We reveal unto thee (O Mohammad!) by inspiration; thou was not with them when they cast lots with arrows as to which of them should be charged with the care of Mary; nor was thou with them when they disputed (the point). Behold! the angels said "O Mary! God giveth thee glad tidings of a Word from him: his name will be Christ (Messiah) Jesus the son of Mary held in honor in this world and the hereafter and of (the company of) those nearest to God. He shall speak to the people in childhood and in maturity and he shall be (of the company) of the righteous." She said: "O my lord! how shall I have a son when no man hath touched me?" He said: "Even so: God createth what He willeth; when He hath decreed a plan He but saith to it `Be' and it is! And God will teach him the Book and Wisdom, the Law and the Gospel. And (appoint him) an Apostle to the Children of Israel (with this message): "I have come to you with a sign from your Lord in that I make for you out of clay as it were the figure of a bird and breathe into it and it becomes a bird by God's leave; and I heal those born blind and the lepers and I quicken the dead by God's leave; and I declare to you what ye eat and what ye store in your houses. Surely therein is a sign for you if ye did believe.(I have come to you) to attest the Law which was before me and to make lawful to you part of what was (before) forbidden to you; I have come to you with a sign from your Lord. So fear God and obey me. It is God who is my Lord and your Lord; then worship him. This is a way that is straight". (Holy Quran 3:42–51)

Ibn Hazam, a famous Islamic scholar of Muslim Spain who encouraged literal understanding of Quranic text, was of the opinion that as Mary did speak to an angel, which is one of the requirements to qualify as a prophet, she should be seen as a prophetess. He also believed that Sarah, wife of Prophet Abraham (PBUH), was also a prophetess as she also spoke to an angel. Though his opinion is quite a rational one, unfortunately it did not gain acceptance in Muslim societies where the majority believe that prophet-hood is given to men only.

Coming back to the Quranic story of Jesus's birth, the Holy Quran further says in Chapter Mary,

Relate in the Book (the story of) Mary when she withdrew from her family to a place in the East. She placed a screen (to screen herself) from them: then We sent to her Our angel and he appeared before her as a man in all respects. She said: "I seek refuge from thee to (God) Most Gracious:

(come not near) if thou dost fear God." He said: "Nay I am only a messenger from thy Lord (to announce) to thee the gift of a holy son." She said: "How shall I have a son seeing that no man has touched me and I am not unchaste?" He said: "So (it will be): thy Lord saith "That is easy for Me: and (We wish) to appoint him as a Sign unto men and a Mercy from Us: it is a matter (so) decreed." So she conceived him and she retired with him to a remote place. And the pains of childbirth drove her to the trunk of a palm-tree: she cried (in her anguish): "Ah! would that I had died before this! Would that I had been a thing forgotten and out of sight!" But (a voice) cried to her from beneath the (palm-tree): "Grieve not! for thy Lord hath provided a rivulet beneath thee;" And shake towards thyself the trunk of the palm-tree: it will let fall fresh ripe dates upon thee. So eat and drink and cool (thine) eye. And if thou dost see any man say `I have vowed a fast to (God) Most Gracious and this day will I enter into no talk with any human being'. At length she brought the (baby) to her people carrying him (in her arms). They said: "O Mary! Truly an amazing thing hast thou brought"! "O sister of Aaron! Thy father was not a man of evil nor thy mother a woman unchaste"! But she pointed to the baby (Jesus). They said: "How can we talk to one who is a child in the cradle?" He (baby Jesus started speaking miraculously and) said: "I am indeed a servant of God: He hath given me revelation and made me a prophet; And He hath made me blessed wheresoever I be and hath enjoined on me Prayer and Charity as long as I live; (He) hath made me kind to my mother and not overbearing or miserable; So Peace is on me the day I was born the day that I die [on his 2nd coming] and the Day that I shall be raised up to life (again)"! Such (was) Jesus the son of Mary: (it is) a statement of truth about which they (vainly) dispute. It is not befitting to (the majesty of) God that He should beget a son. Glory be to him! When He determines a matter He only says to it "Be" and it is. Verily God is my Lord and your Lord: him therefore serve ye: this is a way that is straight. (Holy Quran 19:16–37)

And it was indeed a miracle that Jesus Christ spoke from the cradle, which was definitely the need of the hour as Mary's chastity was questioned by the people who started raising the finger of blame and accused her of having an illegitimate relationship. Unfortunately, despite seeing all of the miracles, what the disbelievers did not comprehend was the obvious sign of omnipotence of God, who earlier had created Adam without father and mother and created Eve out of a man's side.

The Holy Quran further elaborates this point: "This similitude of Jesus before God is as that of Adam: He created him from dust then said to him: "Be" and he was. The truth (comes) from God alone; so be not of those who doubt" (Holy Quran 3:59–63).

Hagia Sophia in Istanbul is the oldest surviving church, built by Emperor Justinian I in 537 CE. The Ottoman conqueror Sultan Mehmet in 1453 converted it into the royal mosque. In 1934, President Kamal Attaturk secularized it into the Ayasophia museum, prayer rugs have been removed, and with the removal of Islamic calligraphy, the ancient Christian drawings and motifs are emerging on the walls and ceilings.

As I mentioned earlier, the exact date of the Nativity is not known to religious scholarship. A few passages are frequently quoted from Luke's Gospel, which points to a certain season and is a source of controversy even within the Christian community. It reads that at the time of the Nativity,

> …there were in the same country shepherds abiding in the field, keeping watch over their flock by night. And, lo, the angel of the Lord came upon them, and the glory of the Lord shone round about them: and they were sore afraid. And the angel said unto them, Fear not: for, behold, I bring you good tidings of great joy, which shall be to all people. For unto you is born this day in the city of David a savior, which is Christ the lord. (Holy Bible, KJV Luke 2:8–11)

To the critical Christian scholarship "the shepherds grazing their cattle out in the open fields at night" implies that it must be one of the hot starry summery nights and not the white snowy cold nights of December as has been told traditionally. Even to this day the tradition is alive that the shepherds residing in Palestine sent out their flocks into the mountainous and desert regions during the summer months and took them up during late October and early November when the cold weather starts.

The Quran also testifies to the fact that Jesus Christ was born during the months of summer with a beautiful clue hidden in the following verses:

> So she (Mary) conceived him and she retired with him to a remote place. And the pains of childbirth drove her to the trunk of a palm-tree: she cried (in her anguish): "Ah! Would that I had died before this! Would that I had been a thing forgotten and out of sight!" But (a voice) cried to her from beneath the (palm-tree): "Grieve not! for thy Lord hath provided a rivulet beneath thee; "And shake towards thyself the trunk of the palm-tree: it will let fall fresh ripe dates upon thee" (Chapter Mary, 19:16–25).

People from predominantly hot climates like the Middle East, Iran, India, and Pakistan are well aware of the fact that the dates ripen during the summer season and here the Bible and Quran are in agreement that Jesus Christ, the mighty messenger of God, was born not in December but sometime during the months of summer.

Regardless of religious differences in the details of the Nativity, one thing common to Muslims and Christians is the belief in Jesus Christ. Accepting the religious differences as they are, Muslims should actively participate in their communities helping the less fortunate and thus keeping the message of both Prophet Mohammad and Jesus Christ alive.

11. The Pope's Controversial Statement

In 2006, Pope Benedict XVI stepped into a controversy when he quoted the fourteenth century Byzantine Emperor Manuel II Palaeologus: "Show me just what Mohammad brought that was new, and there you will find things only evil and inhuman, such as his command to spread by the sword the faith he preached." The Pope concluded by saying "Violence is incompatible with the nature of God and the nature of the soul" (September 2006).

It is important to understand that the Pope's argument stemmed from the typical Christian understanding that the Christian God is God of mercy and love, whereas the God of Judaism as well as of Islam is a vengeful, warring God. Therefore, in Christian literature there are frequent references to Jesus Christ's teaching, "Do not resist one who is evil. But if anyone strikes you on the right cheek, turn to him the other also." (Holy Bible Matt. 5:39).

However, none of the Abrahamic faiths—Islam, Christianity, or Judaism—are toothless religions. I suggest the Pope read the history of the Crusades when the Church used the sword to further its cause, citing these words of Jesus Christ, "As for these enemies of mine, who did not want me to reign over them, bring them here and slay them before me" (Luke 19:27). Not only that, but throughout the Church's history thousands of "Christian heretics," too, were put to the sword, especially during the infamous Inquisitions, using these same words.

Jesus also said that we should "first take the log out of our own eye and then we shall see clearly to take the speck out of our brother's eye" (Matt.7:5). In a time when the relations between the Muslim and the Christian world are extremely tense, the Pope's statement may add fuel to the fire. Therefore, it is important that we all are reasonable and respectful of each other's religion.

12. The Pope's Visit to the Blue Mosque

God Almighty in the Holy Quran says, "Nearest to the Muslims in love wilt thou find those who say, 'We are Christians': Because amongst them are men devoted to learning and men who have renounced the world, and they are not arrogant" (Holy Quran 5:85).

Time and again Muslims have witnessed the truth of these divine words, and most recently, the referenced humility was shown by Pope Benedict XVI when the pontiff paused in silent prayer during his visit to the famous Blue Mosque in Istanbul, Turkey (November 30, 2006).

Standing alongside the Mufti of Istanbul, the Pope faced Makkah and adopted the posture of Muslim prayer with his forearms crossed above the naval, showing his respect to the second largest world religion after Christianity. According to the Vatican's official website the Pope is trying to reach out to Muslims; in Istanbul he tried to mend the fences after offending the Muslim world with the comments he made in September 2006.

It is time for Muslims, too, to move forward and establish a relationship with the Christian world based on respect for each other's point of view and religion.

It is important to recall that Prophet Mohammad (PBUH) interacted congenially with the Christians of his time. We know from the history books that the Prophet had meetings and dealings with several Christians, including Waraqah bin Nawfal, a Christian scholar of Makkah; Bohira, a monk of Syria; and the Christians of Najran from Southern Arabia. The willingness on the part of the Abyssinian king, Negus, to accept Muslims as immigrants in his land during the Makkan period of the Prophet's ministry was also proof of significant interaction between the Christian king and the Prophet.

The most significant interaction between the Christians and the Prophet was the visit of a Christian delegation of Najran to Madina. This period of history can serve to guide contemporary Muslims as to what a "dialogue" between Christians and Muslims should be like. Prophet Mohammad had been sending official letters to different countries and their rulers, inviting them to accept Islam, and Najran was no exception.

At that time the Christians of Najran had a highly organized religious society, and a few among them had converted to Islam. Their conversion aroused the interest of their elders, who wanted to know what the new religion, Islam, was all about. A small delegation of scholars was dispatched from Najran to Madina with the sole purpose of learning the nature of the revelations that Prophet Mohammad received.

Prophet Mohammad warmly welcomed the delegation and arranged their stay in Madina in a secure place close to his mosque. The Prophet also allowed them to pray in Masjid al-Nabawi where the Muslims prayed, a gesture somewhat similar to the Pope's present-day experience in Istanbul. Even though Islam and Christianity share many commonalities in Christology, including Jesus's miraculous birth, his prophethood, his miracles, including his ascension to Heaven, and a belief in his second coming, what makes them different is the Christians' belief of Jesus's divine essence and therefore of trinity. It is needless to say that though the debating parties were not able to reach a consensus in theological terms, the delegation's visit signified the first peaceful dialogue between

Christians and Muslims. It also demonstrated the open-heartedness of the Prophet, who allowed the Christian delegation to pray in his mosque.

Accepting theological differences "as they are" was the first step in establishing peaceful relations between the Christians and Prophet Mohammad some fourteen hundred years ago. Despite their disagreements, both parties were able to pen a social pact keeping the larger good of humanity in mind. It is through the Prophet's Sunnah (act) we learn that Islam teaches primacy of peaceful co-existence with other religious communities. Needless to say, what we need the most today is a similar gesture of goodwill.

13. Did Jesus Live 100 BCE?

According to Christian scholarship today, the date of Jesus Christ's birth cannot be placed with certainty. For many it might seem obvious that Jesus must have been born in the year 1 of the Common Era (CE) or Anno Domini (AD). But as the Christian calendar was developed five hundred years later by a monk named Dionysius, who apparently miscalculated it by around four years, the birth of Christ today is believed to have happened in 4 BCE. Because all Christian references for Christ's birth are from the New Testament most people believe that it happened when Romans ruled. If you believe that it was the Roman era, as the New Testament suggests, it becomes logical to follow the subsequent events in his ministry from the Bible, including his arrest, trial, and crucifixion, assuming a collaborative effort between the Romans and a group of certain Jews of his time.

Many Muslim scholars entertain the Christian account of Christ's suffering as a possibility, but as the Holy Quran explicitly states that Jesus was "neither killed nor crucified" these Muslim scholars believe that someone else might have taken the place of Christ to suffer the torment on the cross. This was, in fact, a minority opinion among a few early Christian sects and somehow in the course of history became a Muslim opinion.

If you ask these Muslim sources when, exactly, the substitution occurred you will find a variety of opinions about it. Some believe it happened in a room before Jesus's arrest when his likeness was put on one of his disciples who volunteered (referring to the fabricated Gospel of Barnabas); others may say it happened when he was carrying the cross en route to crucifixion; yet still others say it happened on the cross.

For the sake of discussion, let me divide the evidence we have about Christology into two groups. One is, of course, the "Western" Roman Catholic account, which influenced the Eastern Orthodox Church as well as all the Protestant churches. The other evidence we have I will refer to as the "Eastern," comprising the Jewish accounts called "Talmud" and Muslim accounts, known as the Holy Quran.

Because the Talmudic account of Jesus and his mother are somewhat hostile in nature many Christians try to refrain from discussing those. But without repeating the allegations of Talmud there seems to be an important sentence in it stating "Jesus appeared during the time of Alexander Janneus", roughly 100 BCE, the second last Jewish King of Maccabee family, who ruled with an iron fist. History has recorded that he ordered the crucifixion of eight hundred rabbis in a single day because of religious differences. Even though the Talmud was written 200–600 CE, at a time when Christian-Jewish schism was at its height, the rabbis did not mention any part the Romans played in the alleged trial and crucifixion of Jesus Christ, even though blaming others could have saved their own necks from Christian persecution. Instead, they boasted in the Talmud that Jesus was killed at the hands of Jews. That makes me inclined to believe that maybe it was in fact the real time period (100 BCE) when Jesus actually appeared.

Similarly, the Holy Quran does not mention a single word of Roman involvement; rather as in the Talmud the story remains purely a Jewish matter.

The Holy Quran says,

> The People of the Scripture (Jew) ask of thee
> (Mohammad) that thou shouldst cause an (actual) Book

to descend upon them from heaven. They asked a greater thing of Moses aforetime, for they said: Show us God plainly. The storm of lightning seized them for their wickedness. Then (even after that) they chose the calf (for worship) after clear proofs (of God's Sovereignty) had come unto them. And We forgave them that! And We bestowed on Moses evident authority.

And We caused the Mount to tower above them at (the taking of) their covenant: and We bade them: Enter the gate, prostrate! and We bade them: Transgress not the Sabbath! and We took from them a firm covenant.

Then because of their breaking of their covenant, and their disbelieving in the revelations of God, and their slaying of the Prophets wrongfully, and their saying: Our hearts are hardened, Nay, but God hath set a seal upon them for their disbelief, so that they believe not save a few.

And because of their disbelief and of their speaking against Mary a tremendous calumny;

And because of their saying: We slew the Messiah Jesus son of Mary, God's messenger; They slew him not nor crucified him, but the matter was made dubious unto them; and lo! those who disagree concerning it are in doubt thereof; they have no knowledge thereof save pursuit of a conjecture ; they slew him not for certain,

But God took him up unto Himself. God was ever mighty, wise. (Holy Quran 4:153–159)

If we rely on the Jewish and Quranic accounts it becomes clear that Jesus was born not in the Roman era but at a time when Jews were the rulers in Judea. Also, as the Holy Quran does not support "substitution theory," and neither can we find any authentic hadith from Prophet Mohammad on this matter, it is safe to conclude that it was the personal opinions of a few second and third generation early Muslim converts who might have borrowed it from different Christian sects of Asia Minor.

And God knows best.

14. Was Jesus God?

In the Holy Quran, God Almighty in Chapter Mary says

> They (Christians) say: "(God) Most Gracious has begotten a son!" Indeed ye have put forth a thing most monstrous! As if the skies are ready to burst the earth to split asunder and the mountains to fall down in utter ruin. That they should invoke a son for (God) Most Gracious. For it is not consonant with the majesty of (God) Most Gracious that He should beget a son. Not one of the beings in the heavens and the earth but must come to (God) Most Gracious as a servant. He does take and account of them (all) and hath numbered them (all) exactly. And every one of them will come to him singly on the Day of Judgment. On those who believe and work deeds of righteousness will (God) Most Gracious bestow Love. (Holy Quran 19:88–96)

After refuting this unjust claim of our Christian brethren, the Holy Quran further says

O people of the Book! Commit no excesses in your religion: nor say of God aught but truth. Christ Jesus the son of Mary was (no more than) an Apostle of God and His Word which He bestowed on Mary and a Spirit proceeding from Him: so believe in God and His Apostles. Say not "Trinity": desist: it will be better for you: for God is One God: glory be to him: (far Exalted is He) above having a son. To Him belong all things in the heavens and on earth. And enough is God as a Disposer of affairs. Christ disdaineth not to serve and worship God nor do the angels those nearest (to God): those who disdain His worship and are arrogant He will gather them all together unto himself to (answer). But those who believe and do deeds of righteousness He will give their (due) rewards and more out of His bounty: but those who are disdainful and arrogant He will punish with a grievous penalty; nor will they find besides God any to protect or help them. (Holy Quran 4:172–173)

Not only Christians, but some Jewish sects of ancient Arabia, too, ascribed a son to God Almighty:

The Jews call Uzair (Ezra) a son of God and the Christians call Christ the son of God. That is a saying from their mouths; (in this) they but imitate what the unbelievers of old used to say. God's curse be on them: how they are deluded away from the truth!
They take their priests and their rabbis to be their lords in derogation of God and (they take as their Lord) Christ the son of Mary; Yet they were commanded to worship but one God: there is no god but He. Praise and glory to him: (far is He) from having the partners they associate (with Him). (Holy Quran 9:30–31)

In a Qudsi hadith (prophetic tradition), Prophet Mohammad (PBUH) said: God Almighty says, "The son of Adam accuses me, and he should not do that. He claims that I have a son, but

I am the One and the Only, the Eternal and Absolute, I (God) begets not, nor was I begotten and there is none comparable to Me." (*Sahih Bukhari*).

Therefore one can understand why the Quran takes a strong exception to polytheistic ideas.

> In blasphemy indeed are those that say that God is Christ the son of Mary. Say: "Who then hath the least power against God if His Will were to destroy Christ the son of Mary, his mother and all everyone that is on the earth? For to God, belongeth the dominion of the heavens and the earth and all that is in between. He createth what He pleaseth. For God hath power over all things." (Holy Quran 5:17)

We find further elaboration on this point in chapter Al-Maidah, which refutes the concept of Trinity by saying

> They do blaspheme who say: "God is Christ the son of Mary." But said Christ (himself): "O children of Israel! Worship God my Lord and your Lord". Whoever ascribes divinity to any being beside God, God will forbid him the heavens and the fire will be his abode. There will for the wrong-doers be no one to help. They do blaspheme who say: "God is one of three in a Trinity": for there is no god except One God. If they desist not from their word (of blasphemy) verily a grievous penalty will befall the blasphemers among them. Why turn they not to God and seek His forgiveness? For God is Oft-forgiving Most Merciful. Christ the son of Mary was no more than an Apostle; many were the Apostles that passed away before him. His mother was a woman of truth. They had both to eat their (daily) food. See how God doth makes His Signs clear to them; yet see in what ways they are deluded away from the truth! (Holy Quran 5:72–75)

The Holy Quran sketches a scene from the Day of Judgment, and to refute the Christian idea of the "divine son," the Holy Quran presents a conversation that will occur between Jesus Christ and God Almighty:

> And behold! God will say "O Jesus the son of Mary! Didst thou say unto men "worship me and my mother as gods in derogation of God"? He will say: "Glory to Thee! never could I say what I had no right (to say). Had I said such a thing Thou wouldst indeed have known it. Thou knowest what is in my heart though I know not what is in Thine. For Thou knowest in full all that is hidden. Never said I to them aught except what Thou didst command me to say to wit `Worship God my Lord and your Lord'; and I was a witness over them whilst I dwelt amongst them; when Thou didst take me up thou wast the Watcher over them and Thou art a Witness to all things. If Thou dost punish them they are Thy servants: if Thou dost forgive them Thou art the Exalted the Wise." God will say: "This is a day on which the truthful will profit from their truth: theirs are gardens with rivers flowing beneath their eternal home: God well-pleased with them and they with God: that is the great salvation (the fulfillment of all desires). To God doth belong the dominion of the heavens and the earth and all that is therein and it is He who hath power over all things." (Holy Quran 5:116–120)

15. Was Christ Crucified?

The answer to this question is a categorical no, as Muslims are told in the Holy Quran:

> They [Jews of Talmud] said (in boast), "we killed Christ Jesus the son of Mary, the messenger of Allah." But they killed him not, nor crucified him, but the matter was made dubious to them, and those who differ therein are full of doubts, with no (certain) knowledge, but only conjecture to follow, for of surety they killed him not. Nay, Allah raised him up unto himself; and Allah is exalted in power, wise. (Holy Quran 4:157–158)

In this essay we will examine the issue of confusion and doubt that surrounds the events related to the last days of his ministry, especially just before his ascension.

Let us first review the Christian ideology of the crucifixion, death, and resurrection of Jesus, which is based on Paul's preaching. Paul is the most influential writer in New Testament, with more than half of its books attributed to him. Pauline Christology started with a letter he wrote to the people of Corinth:

> For I delivered unto you first of all that which I also received, how that Christ died for our sins according to the scriptures; And that he was buried, and that he rose again the third day according to the scriptures: And that he was seen of Cephas, then of the twelve: After that, he was seen of above five hundred brethren at once; of whom the greater part remain unto this present, but some are fallen asleep. After that, he was seen of James; then of all the apostles. And last of all he was seen of me also, as of one born out of due time. (1 Cor. 15:3–8)

Furthermore, Paul was the first among the New Testament writers who taught that "if Christ has not been raised, your faith is futile; you are still in your sins" (1Cor. 15:17). It was years later in the evolution of Christian theology that the four Gospel writers, working with the plot provided by Paul, came up with a colorful story of how the alleged "passion-resurrection" event happened.

Modern day scholars tell us that the oldest manuscripts of the New Testament, famously called Codex Sinaiticus, Codex Vaticanus, and Codex Alexandrinus, all date around the fourth or fifth century CE. Scholars believe that Paul's letter can be dated around 50–60 CE, the Gospels of Mark 75 CE, Matthew 85–90 CE, Luke and Acts 85–90 CE, and John 95–125 CE. None of the writers of the alleged passion-resurrection narrative were eyewitnesses to the event, and the oldest writer, Paul, never saw, met, or touched Jesus while he walked on this earth.

Moreover, there is scholarly consensus that among the Gospels Mark might have originated independently, whereas Luke and Matthew copied wholesale from Mark (synoptic gospels). As for John, he is independent of the synoptics for the miracles and sayings of Jesus but not for the passion and resurrection stories. These scholars tell us that Matthew and Luke also consulted another major work (the Q Gospel, 50 CE) along with Mark to finalize their account of gospels, yet there is not a single hint about any passion-resurrection story from the Q Gospel.

It is important to realize that Paul's ideology of "salvation related to a belief in death and resurrection of a divine savior" was in itself the dominating religious dogma known to the heathen nations of his times, as Paul himself admits that well before he became a minister "the gospel which you heard, which has been preached to every creature under heaven, and of which I, Paul became a minister." (Col.1:23)

More than a dozen such saviors are known to current biblical scholars, such as Krishna of India (1200 BCE), Thammuz of Syria (1160 BCE), Quexalcote of Mexico (587 BCE), Atys of Phyrygia (1170 BCE), Mithra of Persia, and Buddha of India (600 BCE) to name a few (Kersey Graves. *The world's sixteen crucified saviors* 102–133).

We know from Luke that Paul was born in Tarsus (Acts 21:39; 22:3), an important city of Cilicia in the modern south central Turkey. Hyam Maccoby rightly points out that "In Tarsus his education would have been with pagan children, and his imagination would have been impressed by the beautiful pagan ceremonies of mourning and joy associated with the death and resurrection of certain pagan gods worshipped in Tarsus" (*The Mythmaker: Paul and the Invention of Christianity* 96–97).

It was the genius of Paul coupled with his political ambitions that he successfully presented his Jewish religion in such terms that it became acceptable and palatable to the non-Jewish nations surrounding his people in the land of Judea. According to Paul's own admission, the people of Corinth, doubted him and "desire proof that Christ is speaking in me" and also that, "I was crafty, you say, and got the better of you by guile" (2 Cor. 13 and 14). In the book of Romans (3:7) Paul admits that he did not hesitate to use deceit in his conversion process: "But if through my falsehood God's truthfulness abounds to his glory, why am I still being condemned as a sinner?" With his own confession it is clear to me that in the purest terms he was a politician who was led by the assumption that the end justifies the means, and by doing so he discredited his own "lord and savior" Jesus Christ, who taught that it is only the truth that sets anybody free (John 8:32).

It was in this religious and cultural context that Jesus Christ was born miraculously as a sign from God Almighty, revealing to these heathen nations in general, and Jews in particular, that a miraculous birth in itself does not qualify a divine status. Rather, it is just like any other ordinary birth, with dependency on a mother to give birth and breast feed and change the diapers afterward, something that God Almighty does not require.

The Holy Quran testifies to these facts in these simple terms as follows:

> The similitude of Jesus before God is as that of Adam; He created him from dust, then said: "Be" and he was. The truth comes from thy Lord alone; so be not of those who doubt. (3:59–60)
> Christ, the son of Mary was no more than a messenger: many were the messengers that passed away before him, his mother was a woman of truth. They had both to eat their (daily) food. See how God doth make His signs clear to them; yet see in what ways they are deluded away from the truth! (5:75)

It is clear from the historic accounts that at some point during the ministry of Jesus the Jewish unbelievers of his time, threatened by his call of religious reformation and afraid of losing their own positions in the community, planned to harm him and God made Jesus aware of his future ascension well in advance, as the Holy Quran tells us

> And (the unbelievers) plotted and planned, and God too planned, and the best of planners is God. Behold! God said: O Jesus! I will take thee and raise thee to myself and clear thee (of the falsehood) of those who blaspheme; I will make those who follow thee superior to those who reject faith, to the day of resurrection: then shall ye all return unto me, and I will judge between you of the matters wherein ye dispute. (Holy Quran 3:54–55)

Similarly, the recently discovered "Gospel of Thomas," unearthed in 1945 near Nag Hammadi in Egypt, shows no knowledge of crucifixion of Jesus. It consists exclusively of sayings, parables, and dialogues attributed to Jesus. It reads, "The followers said to Jesus: 'We know that you are going to leave us. Who will be our leader?' Jesus said to them: 'No matter where you are, you are to go to James the Just, for whose sake heaven and earth came into being'" (Thomas 12). Here you find Jesus and his disciples reflecting the knowledge of his future ascension and his disciples' concern about the future leadership of the true Christian community. Clearly, they know that he is not going to come back in the near future, otherwise the logical answer from Jesus would have been "Why do you worry! We have lots of time. I am not leaving until I am crucified and raised to life again and dwelt among you for another forty days from that event"; rather, you find Jesus expressing his will in favor of James in anticipation of his imminent ascension.

For a complete picture, it is important to review Jewish understanding of the events. We are told that "Jesus was a scholar of Joshua Ben Perachiah (who lived a century before the time assigned by the Christians for the birth of Jesus), accompanied him into Egypt, there learned magic, and was a seducer of the people, and finally put to death by being stoned and then hung as a blasphemer," says T.W. Doane in his book *Bible Myths And Their Parallels In Other Religions*. Please note that the Jews were also not clear about the manner of "alleged death" of Jesus, if it was secondary to stoning or hanging (or crucifixion); they also failed to show the dead body or even the grave of Christ, which could have settled the case in their favor.

Paul's imagination (50–60 CE) worked well in favor of crucifixion because of obvious reasons, as I discussed earlier. To strengthen his claim he added the vision of the risen Christ, but failed again to mention the most crucial evidence, indicated by this series of questions: What happened to the dead body of Christ; was he buried in a grave; were there any other witnesses to the event of crucifixion, death, and resurrection of Jesus Christ? These questions must have been a nuisance to the followers of Paul, as they, in subsequent decades (from 80–125 CE), wrote their respective gospels primarily addressing these questions.

Doane rightly remarks that "In the first two centuries the professors of Christianity were divided into many sects, but these might all be resolved into two divisions — one consisting of Nazarenes, Ebionites and Orthodox; the others Gnostics." Gnostics idealized the personality of Jesus to such extremes that his humanity was reduced to a phantom without reality. They generally agreed in saying that Christ was an Aeon, though they admitted the crucifixion, considering it to have happened in some mystical way, but denied that Christ did really die, in the literal meaning of the term, on the cross.

Among the former group we find Paul and his associates, who accepted and propagated the story in literal terms as I discussed earlier. Many other groups from Asia Minor totally rejected the event of crucifixion either in reality or metaphorically and are described by Irenaeus (198 CE); their belief was that Jesus was not crucified at the time stated in the gospels but lived to be nearly fifty years old. Irenaeus also states:

"They could not conceive of the first begotten Son of God being put to death on a cross, and suffering like an ordinary being, so they thought Simon of Cyrene (a passerby who according to gospels was compelled by Romans to carry the cross) must have been substituted for him, as the ram was substituted in place of Isaac." (T.W.Doane, *Bible Myths and Their Parallels in Other Religions* 508–530)

Among the four opinions about Christ's last hours on this earth (one Jewish and three Christian), the substitution theory impressed some of our Muslim scholars too, years after the demise of Prophet Mohammad (PBUH).[1]

In summary, the Christian communities of the Q Gospel and the Gospel of Thomas had no knowledge of the trial, crucifixion, death, and resurrection myth and it naturally follows that their "faith" did not rest on these details at all. The myth of crucifixion was created by Paul, who is the most Jewish-friendly among the New Testament writers and the first to affirm the Jewish claim (in the Talmud) that Jesus Christ was killed, when the fact is that despite all the evil intentions they had against Jesus, they were not able to touch this mighty messenger of God. God Almighty in the Holy Quran says "And behold! I did restrain Bani Israel from (violence to) thee (Jesus), when thou didst show them the clear signs (miracles), and the unbelievers among them said: 'This is nothing but evident magic'" (Holy Quran 5:10).

Further Reading:

1. Jesus Christ and Barabbas

According to all four Gospels, Barabbas was a person chosen by the Jewish crowd in preference to Jesus Christ for the Roman governor Pilate to release on the feast of Passover.

"Therefore when they were gathered together, Pilate said unto them, whom will ye that I release unto you? Barabbas, or Jesus, which is called Christ?" (Matt. 27:17)

"But the chief priests (Jewish) moved the people, that he should rather release Barabbas unto them" (Mark 15:11).

"And they cried out all at once, saying, away with this man (Jesus), and release unto us Barabbas" (Luke 23:18).

"Then cried they all again, saying, Not this man, but Barabbas. Now Barabbas was a robber" (John 18:40).

The literal meaning of this Aramaic name (Bar Abba) is "son of Abba," or "son of father" or "son of God," as Abba or father is a form of an Aramaic word used for "God the father," as we already know from Paul's letters. (Gal. 4:6 and Rom. 8:15).

Now following are some facts I think you might find interesting. In the Anchor Bible dictionary, Vol. 1, under the heading Barabbas you read

> An interesting variant occurs in Mt 27: 16-17, where he is called "Jesus Barabbas." While extant manuscript evidence is weak, Origen implies that most manuscripts in his day (240 CE) included the full name. Many

scholars today accept the full name in Matthew as original and suggest that it was probably omitted by later scribes because of repugnance of having Jesus Christ's name being shared by Barabbas. It is not improbable for Barabbas to have the very common name Jesus. Matthew's text reads more dramatically with two holders of the same name: "Which Jesus do you want; the son of Abba, or the self styled Messiah (Albright and Mann Matthew AB, 343–4). There is some evidence that the full name "Jesus Barabbas" also originally appeared in Mark's gospel. (Mann Mark AB, 637)

Knowing the above facts in detail, the authors of *Hiram Key*, Christopher Knight and Robert Lomas, had this to say:

So the individual who was released and not crucified at the request of the crowd was, as an indisputable matter of Gospel record, known as 'Jesus, the son of God'. The first part of the name was deleted from the gospel of Matthew at a much later date, by those that sought to establish facts to fit their gentile belief. Such selectivity is what we would now euphemistically call "being economical" with the truth, but it is little more than a deceit to avoid difficult questions that the Church would not, or more likely could not answer. The gospel state that this other 'Jesus, the son of God', was accused of being a Jewish rebel who had killed people during an outbreak of insurrection. Thus Barabbas was not a criminal but a Jewish fanatic, one facing a similar accusation to the one brought against Jesus. When these fuller facts are taken into account, the whole circumstances of the trial of Jesus become much more complicated. Two men of the same name with the same claim and much the same crime: How can we know which one was released? Certainly many of the oldest Christian sects believed that Jesus did not die on the cross because another died for him. Muslims today hold Jesus Christ in very high regard as a prophet who was ordered to be crucified but whose place was taken by another. The symbolism of the crucified Christ is absolutely central to main line Christianity, yet so many groups both contemporary to the event and modern hold that he did not die in this manner. Could they be right? (50)

We may never know what *exactly* happened prior to Jesus's ascension, but I'll request my Christian brethren to at least consider the plausibility of the Quranic claim that "Jesus was neither killed nor crucified but the matter was made dubious," as the above references in current Christian scholarship clearly verify what was miraculously revealed to Prophet Mohammad (PBUH) some fourteen hundred years ago.

16. What Is Easter?

Islam has no concept of Easter, as Muslims are told in the Holy Quran that Jesus Christ, the messenger of Allah, was "neither killed nor crucified"; rather Allah ascended him unto Himself, "alive," and saved him from nakedness and a shameful death on the cross. In other words, we do not hold the dogma of "death and resurrection" of Jesus as the bedrock claim for our faith—a basic requirement for the Pauline Church, which claims that

> Christ died for our sins in accordance with the scripture, that he was buried, that he was raised on the third day in accordance with the scripture...If Christ has not been raised, then our preaching is in vain and your faith is in vain...If Christ has not been raised, your faith is futile and you are still in your sins. (Holy Bible, RSV 1 Cor. 15:4–17)

To celebrate this alleged event of death and resurrection of Jesus the Christian world commemorates a day by the name "Easter," a non-biblical term derived from a heathen goddess, Ostart of the Saxons and the Eostre of the Germans. An inquiry into the subject reveals that this Christian festival is developed from the Jewish Passover (Hebrew Pesach) because according to the Christian record, the events of Jesus's last days on earth took place at the time of Passover, that is, the fourteenth of Nisan.

For the Jews, Passover is a religious festival commemorating God's deliverance of the Israelites from Pharaoh's bondage. The month (Nisan) in which it happened was selected by a divine decree as the first month of their lunar yearly cycle (Exod. 12). Some scholars think that the Passover was originally a spring New Year festival mixed with Jewish religious ideologies: the first of Nisan fell on the day after the appearance of the new moon following the vernal equinox, so that the fourteenth of Nisan coincided with the spring full moon and in contradistinction to the planetary and the Julian solar year, had ever-varying dates, and moved in rhythm with the dance of heavenly bodies (Hugo Rahner, *Greek Myths And Christian Mysteries* 110).

It is said that the early Christians did not celebrate the resurrection of Jesus from the grave; rather they celebrated Jewish Passover as their chief festival, celebrating it on the same day as the Jews, on 14 Nisan, believing according to their tradition that Jesus on the eve of his alleged death had eaten the Passover meal with his disciples. They regarded such a solemnity as a commemoration of the supper and not as a memorial of the resurrection.

In the mid second century, however, some gentile Christians began to celebrate it on the Sunday after 14 Nisan with the preceding Friday observed as the day of Christ's alleged death, regardless of the date on which it fell. A very long schism took place in the Christian church and in 197 CE, Victor of Rome excommunicated many of those Christians who insisted on celebrating Easter on 14 Nisan. The dispute continued until the fourth century, when Emperor Constantine in the council of Nicene, confirmed the practice of observing Easter on the Sunday following 14 Nisan, rather than on that date itself.

> The most characteristic Easter rite, and the one most widely diffused, is the use of Easter eggs. They are usually stained of various colors with dye—woods or herbs

and people mutually make present of them, sometimes they are kept as amulets, sometimes eaten. Now, dyed eggs were used as sacred Easter offerings in Egypt; and the ancient Persians used them in their celebration of Solar new year ceremonies which were held in the month of March where people presented each other with colored eggs; the Jews used eggs in feast of Passover and the custom prevailed in the western countries. (T.W. Doane, *Bible Myths And Their Parallels In other Religions* 228)

17. Christian Symbols and Christmas

In the Holy Bible, God clearly told the ancient Israelites that to keep their faith pure they should not associate Him with any of His creations, saying

> Therefore take good heed to yourselves, since you saw no form on the day that the Lord spoke to you at Horeb, out of the midst of the fire, beware lest you act corruptly by making a graven image for yourselves, in the form of any image, the likeness of male or female, the likeness of any beast that is on the earth, the likeness of any winged bird that flies in the air, the likeness of anything that creeps on the ground, the likeness of any fish that is in the water under the earth. And beware lest you lift up your eyes to heaven, and when you see the sun and the moon and the stars, all the host of heaven, you be drawn away and worship them and serve them, things which the Lord your God has allotted to all the peoples under the whole heaven. (Holy Bible, RSV, Deut. 4:15–19)

To put it simply, don't follow the pagans; rather, the worship of imageless, invisible God should be the tenet of one's faith.

In another place we read "You shall not make for yourself a graven image, or any likeness of anything that is in the heaven above, or that is in the earth beneath, or that is in the water under the earth: you shall not bow down to them or serve them; for I the Lord your God am a jealous God" (Exod. 20:4–5).

A similar message one finds in Islam, and beautifully summarized in the Holy Quran

> (He is) the Creator of the heavens and the earth: He has made for you pairs from among yourselves and pairs among cattle: By this mean does He multiply you: There is nothing whatever like unto Him, And He is the One that hears and sees (all things). To Him belong the keys of the heavens and the earth: He enlarges and restricts the sustenance to whom He will: For He knows full well all things. (Holy Quran 42:11–12)

Unfortunately, this simple divine message of monotheism was forgotten many times in the course of history by almost all of the sects in the Abrahamic faiths. We are all equal in ignorance and no different from one another when we call upon the names of Prophets and saints for assistance, instead of God the Creator, and therefore associate them in power and might with Him, the worst kind of sin in all three Abrahamic faiths. Religious history is witness to the fact that it is always the literate ones who lead the unwary to wrongdoings; therefore, Jews required rabbinic rulings; Muslims, scholarly Fatwas; and Christians, their councils and creeds to numb their conscience.

Our Christian brethren under the leadership of Paul corrupted the true message of Jesus Christ and introduced the myth of "death and resurrection of a divine crucified savior for salvation of the world," known to every heathen nation of his times, with clear political intentions. His efforts, supposedly for the glory of God, attracted pagans who found themselves at home, having tons of divine incarnate saviors in their surroundings.

The following example illustrates how a preconceived ideology can change the truth in a totally different direction. Geza Vermes, a famous Jewish scholar, says:

> [The term] "Son of God" was always understood metaphorically in Jewish circles. In Jewish sources, its use never implies participation by the person so named in the divine nature. It may in consequence safely be assumed that if the medium in which Christian theology developed had been Hebrew and not Greek, it would not have produced an incarnation doctrine as this is traditionally understood. (John Hick, *The Metaphor Of God Incarnate* 42–43)

And if you allow me to add here: if the Jews had accepted Jesus and propagated his message instead of the heathen Greco-Roman converts, the result would have been drastically different.

The most perverted ideology from antiquity to the present is the belief in astrology, with the sun as the central figure along  with moon, five planets in ancient times, and twelve signs of zodiac. This pseudoscience is based on erroneous assumption that the earth is the center of the universe and all planets and the luminaries revolve around it (geocentricity), contrary to what we know today of the nature of the universe. The zodiac signs are remarkably similar in different cultures and most scholars believe that their origin is from ancient Babylon and Mesopotamia. In short, the movement of the sun in different zodiacal signs was supposed to influence human affairs. That is how divinity was imparted to them.

Without going into the jargon of astrology, a little introduction is necessary to understand what I'll elaborate later. The ancient astronomers inscribed an imaginary central line representing the ecliptic, or apparent orbit of the sun around the earth and then divided it into 360 degrees. Quartering these to denote the seasons, they named the cardinal points the Summer and Winter Solstices, and Vernal and Autumnal Equinoxes; the former referred to the longest and shortest days of the year; the latter to the two periods when the days and nights are equal.

The other imaginary belt of importance is known as orbit of the zodiac, or the celestial equator, in which the twelve constellations or signs of the zodiac revolve around the earth. This orbit intersects the ecliptic (sun's orbit) at a certain angle, giving the ancients the idea of heavenly cross. The most famous reference to this cross formed by the ecliptic and the celestial equator is found in Plato's dialogue *"Timaeus,"* where Plato tells us how Demiurge (the creator of universe in Greek mythology) constructed the universe out of two circles that he joined "in the form of the letter X" (David Ulansey, *The Origins Of The Mithraic Mysteries* 47).

To the pagans of antiquity it was known that the sun moves backward through the zodiac, one degree every seventy-two years, so that every 2,160 years the spring point, or vernal equinox, slips into a new zodiacal sign. That is why we see the cult of Taurus (Bull) flourishing in ancient Egypt, 4000–2000 BCE, which the Israelites later worshipped in the form of a golden calf. During the age of Aries, 2000–1 BCE, the ram became prevalent in ancient religious symbolism; an example is the ram-headed solar god Amen-Ra in Egypt. Finally, the era of Pisces, 1–2000 CE, heralds the birth of Christianity and its prevalent fish symbolism. In the 1980s the equinox moved out of the constellation of Pisces and into Aquarius, where it will remain for another 2,160 years. If Jesus Christ had been born in our times, the symbol of Christianity would have been the sign of the water bearer, if one can imagine.

According to the Talmud, his mother gave him the quite common name Yeschu, meaning "the help of Yahweh"; the Greeks made this into Iesous, the Romans into Jesus. The Greek word for the fish is, i-ch-th-u-s, formed after the initials of the phrase "Iesous Christos Theou Uios Soter" — "Jesus Christ, Son Of God, Savior." He was seen both as the "Lamb of God" whose sacrifice closed the era of Aries, and the rising sun of the Piscean era, the celestial fish of a new age (David Fideler, *Jesus Christ, Sun Of God* 160–169).

The early writers were so mesmerized with these astrological myths that his disciples were known as "fishers of men" while the early Christians were known as "little fishes" (Mark 1:17 and Matt. 4:19).

The next symbol is the cross, which made its debut a little late in the evolution of Christianity. We know from the religious history that the cross was used as a religious emblem many centuries before the Christian era, by every nation in the world who believed in a "divine crucifixion." Perhaps to keep themselves unique, despite obvious similarities, the early Christians hesitated to adopt this symbol.

Doane says

> Few cases have been more powerful in producing mistakes in ancient history, than the idea, hastily taken by Christians in all ages that every monument of antiquity marked with a cross, or with any of those symbols which they conceived to be monogram of their god, was of Christian origin. The early Christians did not adopt it as one of their symbols; it was not until Christianity began to be paganized that it became a Christian monogram, and even then it was not the cross, as we know it today. It is not until the middle of fifth century that the pure form of the cross emerges to light. The Labarum cross of Constantine was nothing more than the overlapping X and P (first two Greek letters of the word "Christ" (Greek: ΧΡΙΣΤΟΣ, or Χριστός) — *Chi* (χ) and *Rho* (ρ)), the monogram of Egyptian god Osiris, and afterwards of Christ. (*Bible Myths and Their Parallels in World Religions* 349)

He further states that

> The oldest representation of Jesus Christ was a figure
> of a lamb, to which sometimes a vase was added, into
> which his blood flowed, and at other times couched
> at the foot of a cross. This custom subsisted up to the
> year 680, and until the pontificate of Agathon, during
> the reign of Constantine Pogonat. By the sixth synod of
> Constantinople (canon 82) it was ordained that instead
> of the ancient symbol, which had been the Lamb, the fig-
> ure of a man fastened to a cross (such as the pagans had
> adored), should be represented. All this was confirmed
> by Pope Adrian I. (202)

Now about Christmas we find that nearly all the pagan nations
of antiquity celebrated on December 25th the birth of the god
Sol (sun), which upon incarnation personified into human form
and was considered a divine savior according to the myths.
Tons of such incarnations and saviors are scattered in the religious history of the mankind. To name a few we find Buddha
in India and China, Mithra in Persia, Horus in Egypt, Bacchus
in Thrace and Adonis in Bethlehem. Even in Rome, at the seat
of Catholicism and well before the time of Christ, a festival
was observed on December 25th under the name of Natalis
Solis Invicti, which meant the birth of the sun the invincible
(T.W.Doane, *Bible Myths And Their Parallels In Other Religions*,
359-367).

One wonders what is so special about this date and why did
the genii of ancient religions dedicated a day for the birth of the
sun? Here again the mythologies related to the cardinal points
of Summer and Winter Solstices, and Vernal and Autumnal
Equinoxes come into play. To the ancient mind winter solstice
was considered the most important day among the four, as it
is on that day, the days begin to lengthen with supposed sun's
triumphs over the darkness. To the modern astrologers it is
accepted that in the northern hemisphere winter solstice occurs
on December 21st but to the ancient religious astrologers it

fell on January 6th if you followed the Egyptian astrology and December 25th if you followed the old Julian calendar (Hugo Rahner, *Greek Myths And Christian Mystery*,141).

That is why we see the ancient Eastern churches celebrating the nativity of Jesus Christ on January 6th and the Western churches commemorating it on December 25th. It is interesting to know that "the Eastern churches clung for a time to January 6th and charged their Western brethren with sun worship and idolatry, but by the end of the fourth century December 25th had been adopted also in the East" (Will Durant, *Caesar And Christ*, 558); excluding the Armenian churches. The term Christmas itself first appeared as early as 1123 CE in old English as 'Cristes maesse' and 'Christmas' by 1568, meaning the Mass of Christ (*Harper Collins Bible Dictionary, Revised Edition*, p177). Among the relics of Christmas the one that you would like to know about is the Christmas tree, without which Christmas is considered incomplete. Depending on one's financial status a person can buy a freshly cut Christmas tree or a plastic model of a tree from the local shopping mall, which people decorate with religious zeal and fervor. The *Encyclopedia Britannica* tells us that use of these evergreen trees served as a symbol of eternal life for the ancient Egyptians, Chinese and Hebrews. Tree worship was common among the pagan Europeans and it seems that this custom survived in the form of Christmas tree after their conversion to Christianity. The typical custom consisted of decorating the house and barn with evergreens at the New Year to scare away the devil and evil spirits.

Santa Claus' name has become sine qua none with Christmas, as the discussion of one without the other is almost impossible. It is understood that Santa Claus and its Dutch variant Sinter Klaus are pronunciation of the name Saint Nicholas who is known to be a purely mythical character whose existence cannot be attested by any historical document. From Europe, the Dutch colonist brought his tradition to New York City in the 17th century from where it was adopted by the English speaking community. According to the Encyclopedia Britannica "his legend of a kind old man was united with old Nordic folktales of a magician who punished naughty children and rewarded good children with present; the resulting image of Santa Claus crystallized in the 19th century, and he has ever since remained the patron of gift giving festival of Christmas".

My dear brothers and sisters, I have summarized for you the historical evolution of Christian symbolism, and it would be superfluous to say that the addition of mythologies to the simple teachings of Jesus Christ has totally changed the real monotheistic message of his ministry.

18. What the Jews Say about Paul

There is a general consensus among Christian scholars that without the teachings of St. Paul the religion of Christianity as we know it today would not have survived, and they are right in this assessment. About half of the books of the New Testament are attributed to him; therefore, it is prudent to investigate the personality of Paul to grasp a better understanding of his ideology.

Some modern scholars have tried to explain the motives Paul might have to spread his brand of Christianity. In that circle some think he was a Gnostic (E. Pagels, *The Gnostic Gospels*) and still others, a person who introduced pagan ideas into Judaism (Hyam Maccoby, *The Mythmaker: Paul and the invention of Christianity*). His motives were also questioned and addressed by ancient Christians:

> Epiphanius, himself orthodox, inform us of the Ebionite 'heresy' who believed that Paul was not a Jew at all, but a Greek who went up to Jerusalem for the purpose of marrying the daughter of a priest. In order to get his girl, he underwent circumcision and became a Jewish convert. Then, when he failed to get the girl, he flew into a rage and

wrote against circumcision and against the Sabbath and the Law. (A. N. Wilson, *Paul: The Mind of the Apostle* 34)

The probability of the above-cited opinion I'll leave to any surviving Ebionite (if there is any) to answer, but it clearly illustrates that the distortion of the original message of Jesus Christ by the Pauline Church was something for which the early Christians directly blamed Paul.

When I started studying comparative religion I noticed that Paul is the only author in New Testament who was clearly friendly to the Jews. It is also observable that he addressed his letters to people living out of Judea and never wrote a single word to the people of Jerusalem, the high priests of Solomon's temple and the alleged killers of Jesus Christ. Because of these observations it remained my opinion that he was never really against Jews, but rather tried to part the bridge between Judaism and the "Savior Cults" surrounding his people in the land of Palestine. He must have been very confused seeing that the "Chosen" people of the Torah, the Jews, were enslaved one after the other by heathen powers: first the Assyrians, then the Babylonians, later the Greeks, and finally the Romans. Paul knew that because of the tribal nature of Judaism it was impossible to come to terms with the opponents of that religion. To change the hostile look of Judaism, he presented his Jewish religion to these pagan nations in terms that were acceptable to their ears, such as "we also have a savior who died and was resurrected for the sins of the world."

All that was just my opinion, which could have been wrong. Fortunately, by the grace of God, I found two interesting references strengthening my suspicion.

The first is from the book *The Second Messiah*, written by Christopher Knight and Robert Lomas, which reads "New Testament scholars have shown evidence that some rabbis in Palestine did accept that it was necessary to present Judaism in a different form which could be appreciated by those nurtured in the tradition of Greco-Roman culture" (6). The second reference is from the *Talmud* (the book of Jewish traditions) about the intentions of Paul, supporting the plausibility of my hypothesis.

The reference from Talmud is a long discourse in which the Jews explained that the miracles performed by Jesus were by his uttering of the words of Shem, and boast that they killed Jesus Christ by hanging him on a cabbage-stalk.

Then the Talmud tells us that

His disciples fled and scattered themselves in the kingdom; three of them [went] to Mount Ararat, three of them to Armenia, three to Rome, the others to other places, and misled the people, but wherever they took refuge, God sent his judgment upon them, and they were slain. But many among the apostates of our people went astray after him; there was strife between them and Israelites… confusion of prayers and much loss of money [for Israel].

Everywhere where the apostates caught sight of the Israelites they said to the Israelites: Ye have slain God's anointed [messiah]! But the Israelites answered them: Ye are children of death, because ye have believed on a false prophet! Nevertheless they went not forth from the community of Israel, and there was strife and contention among them, so that Israel had no peace.

When the wise men of Israel saw this they said: [it is now] thirty years since that rouge (Jesus) was put to death, [and] till now we have no peace with these misguided ones, and this hath befallen us because of the number of our sins, for it is written: They have moved Me to wrath with their not-God [They have moved Me to jealously with that which is not God]; They have provoked Me to anger with their vanities, etc;—that is the Christians, who are not [?naught]; with a base people will I provoke them; that is, the Ishmaelites. The wise said: How long shall the apostates profane Sabbath… and feasts, and slay one another? Let us rather seek for a wise man who may take these erring once out of the community of Israel. It is now thirty years that we have admonished them, but they have not returned to God, because they have taken it into their heads that Yeschu

[Jesus] is the Messiah, and so may they go to destruction and peace be with us.

The wise men agreed on a man whose name was Elijahu, and he was very learned in the scripture, and they said to him: We have agreed, that we will pray for thee, that thou shalt be counted as a good Israelite in the other World. Go, and do good for Israel, and remove the apostates from us, that they may go to destruction!

Elijahu went to Sanhedrin at Tiberias, to Antioch, and made proclamation throughout the whole land of Israel: Whoso believeth on Yeschu let him join himself to me! Then said he to them: I am the messenger [apostle] of Yeschu, who sent me to you, and I will show you a marvel, as Yeschu did. They brought unto him a leper, and he laid his hand upon him, so that he was healed. They brought unto him a lame man, he uttered the Shem, laid his hand on him, and he was healed and stood upon his feet. Forthwith they fell down before him and said: Truly thou art the messenger of Yeschu for thou hast shown us marvels as he did.

Elijahu said to them: Yeschu sendeth you his greeting and saith: I am with my Father in heaven at His right hand, until He shall take vengeance on the Jews, as David said: Sit thou on my right hand, etc. At the same hour they all lamented and added foolishness to their foolishness. Elijahu said to them: Yeschu saith to you: Whosoever will be with me in the other world, let him remove himself from the community of Israel and join himself not to them; for my Father in heaven hath already rejected them and from henceforth requireth not their service, for so said He through Isaiah: Your new moons and feast my soul hateth, etc.

But Yeschu saith to you: Whosoever follow me let him profane the Sabbath, for God hateth it, but instead of it He keepeth the Sunday, for on to it God gave light to His world. And for Passover which the Israelites solemnize, keep yet it on the Feast of Resurrection, for he is risen from his grave; for the Feast of weeks, Ascension, for on to it he is ascended to heaven; for New Year, finding of the Cross; for the Great fast day [Day of atonement], the Feast of the Circumcision; for Chanuka [Feast of lights], Calendae [New year]. The foreskin is naught, circumcision is naught; whosoever will circumcise himself let him be circumcised; whosoever will not circumcise himself let him be not circumcised. Moreover, whatsoever God created in the world, from the smallest gnat to mightiest elephant, pour forth its blood upon the ground and eat it for so it is written: As the green grass have I given you all. If one of them compel you to go a mile, go with him twain; If a Jew smite you on the left side turn to him the right also; if a Jew revile you, endure it and return it not again, as Yeschu endured it; in meekness he showed himself therewith he showed also meekness as he practiced it, that ye might endure all that any should do to you. At the last judgment Yeschu will punish them, but do ye have hope according to your meekness, for so it is written: Seek ye the Lord, all ye meek of the earth, etc. Until he separated them from Israel.

But Elijahu who gave them these laws, the not–good ones did it for the welfare of Israel and Christian call him Paul. After he had introduced these laws and commandments the erring ones separated themselves from Israel and strife ceased. (G. R. S. Mead, *Did Jesus Live 100 BC* 273–276)

One might argue that these passages from the Talmud were written late in the religious history of Judeo-Christianity, but the charges of delayed writing stand true for the books of the New Testament, too, as most of its books were not known for the first 150 years of Christianity. Furthermore, Jews wrote these passages at the height of the Jewish/Christian schism and I see no benefit for them to exonerate Paul if he was not their man, when with the same breath they continued attacking Jesus Christ, the mighty messenger of God.

19. Ancient Mysteries, Jesus Christ and the Terrorism of 9/11

I consider 9/11 a cowardly act of terrorism by which some three thousand people lost their lives. Such acts of killing innocents are condemnable and those responsible deserve swift justice without any regard to their race, religion, or culture. Having said that, it is also important to analyze why terrorists chose the World Trade Center and Pentagon, and not any of the other famous public spots in America. In this article we shall discuss ancient mysteries so as to understand the modus operandi of those involved.

It is important to remind my readers that in almost all pagan religions of antiquity it was assumed that gods lived in places far away from their creations, such as the starry heavens. To reach them people erected pyramids in Egypt and stepped zig-gurats in Sumeria. The Holy Quran mirrors this ancient belief: we are told that Pharaoh in confrontation with Moses told his courtiers to "build me a lofty building that I may mount up to the God of Moses" (Holy Quran 28:38).

 But before any pyramid was constructed, more ancient were the pillars. Such pillars were abundant in Egypt, and when two of these pillars were considered united by a heavenly cross beam the three part structure greeted the rising sun from the East, and thus was considered in perfect harmony with the universe. Jews borrowed this Egyptian mythology and introduced it into the Old Testament. We are told in the Holy Bible that at the entrance of Solomon's temple they constructed two pillars; one of them was called Boaz (meaning strength) and the other Jachin (meaning Yah establishes) (1 Kings 7:15–22 and 2 Chron. 3:16–17).

A system of governance was modeled after this, in which a Priest (Zadok) and a king (David), acting in their respective spheres of influence, were thought to bring heaven and earth closer to each other in a perfect harmony. We know from the Dead Sea scrolls that Jews at around the time of Jesus Christ's appearance were waiting for two Messiahs, one priestly and the other kingly (Vermes, *The Complete Dead Sea Scrolls* 84–90). Some scholars believe that the reason Jewish priesthood rebuked Jesus was because he presented himself as a priestly messiah, whereas they were waiting for a kingly messiah to appear who could deliver them from the Romans. To them, Jesus was not worthy of the title as he was not illuminated enough to understand the ideology of two Messiahs (Knight and Lomas, *Hiram Key*).

As the Bible was later shared by the freemasons we see mythological transformation of its preaching into their symbolism. The two pillars of freemasonry are benevolence and justice, the pillars of humanity, depicted often with the all-seeing eye, a sign of God's providence upon it. It is interesting to note that in ancient Egyptian mythologies Horus' right eye was associated

with Sun god Ra. Sometimes the pillars are replaced by two overlaid equilateral triangles thus forming the six-pointed Star of David. One of the triangles, with its summit reaching the heavens, reflects the king's sphere of influence, and the other one, with its base starting in the heavens and summit reaching the earth, reflects the priestly sphere of influence. Both the Star of David and five pointed star (pentagram) "Seal of Solomon" were considered to have magical powers.

We know that founding fathers of America were freemasons; therefore, it is natural to see the expression of their ideas

in day to day American life. Take for example the dollar sign; you will be able to appreciate by now that its bars reflect two pillars and the letter 'S' is a symbolic expression of the sun. I think the northern and southern orientation of the two towers of the World Trade Center reflected the pillars of ancient mythologies. An analysis of the American one dollar bill itself reveals depictions of imprints from the Seal of the United States. One of the imprints shows its six pointed star with the all-seeing-eye on top of one of the triangles; the other hidden triangle I have highlighted

with red lines for clarification.

I would be dishonest not to describe Muslims' pillars (minarets) and stars, which I believe have their origin in Egyptian mysteries as well. Many of the Muslim countries depict on their flags a five-pointed star (pentagram). More recently, especially from the Middle East, we are seeing a campaign introducing an eight-pointed star, which in my opinion reflects two interlocking cubes (Kabah).

Even the six-pointed star, which many believe to belong exclusively to Jews, has its Muslim equivalent. The famous 786, an erroneously calculated Arabic numerical value of "Bismillah Arrahman Nirrahim"

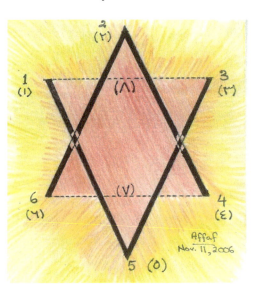

(In the name of God the beneficent the Merciful) is actually a symbolic representation of a six cornered star formed after superimposing the Arabic number seven 'V' with eight 'Λ' with their six corners.

Even though Jews were the first to introduce the concepts of pillars to the Abrahamic faiths, one of their heroes — Samson — was the first to destroy the pillars of their archenemy the Philistines. Cecil B. DeMille made a famous Hollywood movie in 1949 based on the biblical story of Samson and Delilah. The story is narrated in Judges, Chapters 13–16. We are told that Samson was so powerful that he could devour a lion with his bare hands and that he single-handedly killed hundreds of Philistines. The lords of Philistine persuaded their beautiful subject Delilah to "entice him and see wherein his great power lies." After mocking Delilah multiple times, Samson finally admits to her that the secret of his power lies in his long hair, and that if it was cut he would become just like any other man. While he slept, Delilah shaved Samson's hair, and in his weakness he was captured by Philistines, who gouged out his eyes and then brought him to Gaza to grind at a mill in the prison. With the passage of time his hair grew back, and one fine day when the Philistines were celebrating and honoring their fish god Dagon, Samson was called to make sport for the crowd. The Bible says

> Then Samson called to the Lord and said, "O Lord God, remember me, I pray thee, and strengthen me, I pray thee, only this once, O God, that I may be avenged upon the Philistines for one of my two eyes." And Samson grasped the two middle pillars upon which the house rested, and he leaned his weight upon them, his right hand on the one and his left on the other. And Samson said, "Let me die with the Philistines." Then he bowed with all his might: and the house fell upon the lords and upon all the people that were in it.

Even though the terrorism on 9/11was apparently directed against the economic and military might of America, the choice of targets reflect deeper understanding of the Masonic symbolism against which terrorists were operating.

20. The War of the Veils

Generally speaking, Muslim women's veils (face covering) are seen in the Western world as a symbol of oppression and servitude. But for many Muslim women, veiling oneself is an act of righteousness that brings them closer to the teachings of Islam. This self-righteousness at times is boastful and assertive enough to generate a division even within the Muslim communities. The recent effort by the French government to impose a ban on the veil in the public sphere has stirred emotions in the Muslim world. However, many Western countries are expected to follow France's example in the coming days and one could expect more charged discourses on this topic.

Though many contend that the choice whether to wear a veil should be left to an individual, by imposing restrictions the French government is likely to violate women's right of freedom. It also appears to overlook that many Muslim countries such as Saudi Arabia, Iran, and Taliban-controlled Afghanistan rigidly impose the practice of wearing the veil and burqa (cloak) on their female subjects. I once witnessed the enforcement of such harsh practices when a Muslim family was threatened by religious policemen (Mutawwa) in a marketplace in Riyadh,

Saudi Arabia, to either use a veil or go back to their country of origin. In the heat of the argument they asked the shop owner not to do business with the family, thus enforcing a kind of social boycott!

Before we jump to the religiosity of veiling, it will be enlightening to review the culture of the ancient Middle East that the Saudi Mutawwas proudly pointed to. History tells us that veiling of women is not an Islamic innovation, as many mistakenly believe it to be, but was part of the prevailing culture of the avncient Middle East during the times of Prophet Mohammad. Islam, too, had to confront this issue in due course of time.

"Village life in Arabia"

The earliest reference to the veil culture can be cited from Hammurabi's Code. King Hammurabi of Babylon (Iraq) promulgated his laws about eighteen hundred years before Christ, successfully institutionalizing patriarchal control in the family. His laws contain examples of early attempts to regulate and control the activities of the women in Mesopotamia. In subsequent centuries the state became the authoritative force in dictating who among its female subjects must, and must not, wear the veil. By the thirteenth century BCE, Mesopotamian law required that only the elite and free married women should wear a veil, whereas prostitutes and slave women were forbidden to cover their identities. Scholars believe that in those societies the veil was a symbol of respectability and signified that wearer was not available for sexual relationships (Elizabeth Meier, *Women, Crime & Punishment in Ancient Law & Society: The Near East* 130). It is superfluous to say that the laws related to veiling had far reaching implications, especially for subsequent Arab, Persian, and Byzantine civilizations, which practiced it widely.

There is also mention of this practice in Christian writings. Saint Paul wrote to the people of Corinth thus: "Any woman who prays or prophesies with her head unveiled brings shame upon her head (husband), for it is one and the same thing as if she had had her head shaved…she should wear a veil" (1 Cor. 11:3–10). Precisely for this reason we see all depictions of Mary in ancient Christian paintings with her head covered (Hijab). Similarly, ancient Jews who evolved from the same Middle Eastern stock encouraged veiling by the women. Some rabbis even suggested that only one eye should remain exposed, which in their opinion was sufficient for looking at things or people! A recent fatwa (religious ruling) by Saudi clerics sought similar practice of the veil. It is a common sight in Saudi Arabia that veiled female faces — even on advertisement billboards — have one eye painted black with graffiti.

During my student life it puzzled me to see a difference in the outlook of religious prayers and practices between the followers of Islam, Christianity, and Judaism, even though they originated from the same divine source. I now realize that the answer lies in the difference in culture and traditions of ancient Israelites of the Sinai desert, the Christians of Byzantium and Rome, and the Muslims of Arabia that ultimately shaped the persona and outward appearance of these religions. Under cultural pressures all these religions had to make permissible certain norms of one period that in a subsequent era became unacceptable and repugnant. Take, for example, the issue of slavery, which was allowed in almost all ancient cultures and religions at one time or another, but in today's world it is rightly considered the most devilish act. The same is true for female circumcision, which ancient cultures in certain parts of the world practiced with religiosity but in today's world is considered nothing more than a disgusting act of mutilation.

Keeping these facts in mind one should ask exactly what the circumstances in Medina were when the Quranic verses relating to the veil were revealed. In other words, what went wrong should be the focus of our attention for understanding this issue. Two references from *Sahih Bukhari* are worth citing at this juncture and both are self-explanatory.

1. Narrated Hazrat Umar: "I said to Allah's Apostle! Good and bad persons visit you, so I suggest that you order the mothers of the believers (i.e. your wives) to observe veils." Then Allah revealed the verses of Al-Hijab (*Sahih Bukhari*, Vol. 6, hadith number 313).

2. Narrated Hazrat Ayesha (the wife of the Prophet) "Umar bin Al-Khattab used to say to Allah's Apostle 'Let your wives be veiled' but he did not do so. The wives of the Prophet used to go out to answer the call of nature at night only at Al-Manasi (a wilderness outside Madina). Once Sauda (one of the wives of the Prophet), daughter of Zama, went out. She was a tall woman. Umar bin Al-Khattab saw her while he was in a gathering and said, "I have recognized you, O Sauda"! He (Umar) said so as he was anxious for some divine orders regarding the veil (the veiling of women)." So Allah revealed the verses of veiling (*Sahih Bukhari*, Vol. 8, hadith number 257).

It should be clear to readers that the prophet-hood of Hazrat Mohammad (PBUH) created a channel of communication and negotiation between God and the Arabian society of his time. Here Hazrat Umar's suggestion found divine favor, as his intention was to protect the Prophet's family and the early Muslim community. When the Quranic verses were finally revealed, the veil and seclusion were specifically ordained for Prophet's wives to emphasize their special status. In Chapter Al-Ahzab, the veil is a curtain behind which the wives were told to talk to men that were forbidden for them (Holy Quran 33:53). The Holy Quran emphasized that they were not like any other women (Holy Quran 33:32) and should not be treated as such. Seclusion was ordained for them and they were asked not to walk around but stay in their houses (Holy Quran 33:33). The rest of the Muslim women were neither decreed to veil nor were asked to seclude themselves; only to dress modestly, and wrap themselves in their mantles when they walked outdoors, in order to be "recognized" as Muslim women and not be "harassed" (Holy Quran 33:59, 24:31).

Veiling was prescribed and practiced in early Islam as a method of protecting noble ladies from prying eyes and verbal assault: it served as a solution to a social problem of that time and should not be confused as a religious requirement. Modern-day Muslim scholars who see it as a religious obligation should revisit their position. I believe the veil, instead of exposing the full potential of Islam for the entire humanity, is seriously restricting it.

21. Pakistan Should Repeal Its Blasphemy Law

Once again the controversial blasphemy law of Pakistan has made news headlines after the death sentence of Asia Bibi (November, 2010), a Christian mother of five. The prosecution alleged that Ms. Asia made derogatory remarks about Prophet Mohammad (peace be upon him), which carries the death penalty under Section 295-C of the Pakistan Penal Code. The human rights activists of Pakistan are to be commended for their ongoing protest against this controversial legislation since its inception in 1986 by General Zia's regime, as time and again it is exploited for personal enmity and encourages extremism. The following few lines are a rebuttal to the evidence put forward by the proponent of this law.

Historically speaking, just like Christians who once promulgated a similar law to protect the honor of Jesus Christ, this blasphemy law is heavily influenced by the Muslim mentality of the Middle Ages when Islam became the dominant religion in Middle Eastern society. A frequently referenced treatise on this subject by Ibn Taymiyyah (1263–1328 CE), *As-Sarim Al-Maslul ala Shatim Ar-Rasul* (The drawn sword against those who insult the Messenger), was written in response to an incident in which Ibn Taymiyyah saw a Christian insulting Prophet Mohammad.

I invite my readers to further go back in history to the earliest sources and ask a simple question as to what the Prophet himself said and what the Quran teaches about this issue. If the supporters of this law are right, one should see tons of examples in the literature, as throughout his ministry Prophet Mohammad was verbally and physically abused thousands of times. Strangely enough, you find only a few "implied" traditions, exclusively in those books considered less authentic by the scholars such as *Nisai, Abu Dawood,* and *Dar Qutni,* etc. The Holy Quran is completely silent on awarding any worldly punishment on this issue, nor do we find any prophetic tradition (hadith) in its support, especially in the two most authentic books on hadith, *Sahih Bukhari* and *Sahih Muslim.*

The bedrock claim for the proponent of this law is a tradition from *Abu Dawood,* in which a blind man kills his concubine, who used to abuse and disparage the Prophet. She, despite being forbidden many times, according to the blind man's account, did not give up her habit, and one night as she began to slander the Prophet he took a dagger, placed it on her belly, pressed it, and killed her. When the news of this murder reached the Prophet, he confronted the blind man, who in his defense repeated his version of the story. Thereupon the Prophet said: Oh be witness, no retaliation is payable for her blood (*Sunan Abu-Dawood,* hadith number 2048). This concocted tradition is classified by scholars of hadith as Hasan, which linguistically means good and only better than Daif, the weakest tradition. It is important to remind my readers that for early hadith collectors, Muhadiseen, the most important task was to differentiate between Sahih the authentic ones, from Daif traditions. It follows naturally that early Muslims based their faith on Sahih hadiths alone. Scholars tell us that it was Al-Tirmidhi (824–892 CE, 209–279 AH) who in the third century after Hijra became the first to set up rules to identify Hasan traditions among the Daif. Later it became acceptable for use as a religious evidence among scholars, although not rising to the level of Sahih, which is my bias against this kind of tradition. One of the narrators in this tradition, Usman Alsuham, was considered untrustworthy by the hadith scholars (*Mizan Al-Aitdal* 60).

Another tradition with variant reading, considered Daif (weak) by scholars, reads "A Jewess used to abuse the Prophet (peace be upon him) and disparage him. A man strangled her till she died. The Apostle of Allah (peace be upon him) declared that no recompense was payable for her blood" (*Sunan Abu-Dawood*, hadith number 2049). Quite obviously, one would like to know the identity of this blind man, so another variant tradition is pulled out from Ibn Saad's "*Tabqat AlKubra*," where he is identified as Ibn Um al-Maktoom, but this time the female was killed by hitting. Such evidence in a court of law would be instantly thrown out if the witnesses are not clear about the details of the crime.

Once this is settled, the proponents of the blasphemy law present the story related to a death warrant issued by the Prophet against Kab Ashraf, a member of the Jewish tribe of Banu Nadir, who were settlers in the outskirts of Madinah. Before we discuss the circumstances of his murder, it is important to recall that the Prophet as a statesman had given this tribe a charter of freedom and in return they were expected to be loyal to the Muslim State of Madinah. Kab, at some stage, became openly hostile to Islam. He besmirched in verses the reputation of Muslim women and incited the tribes in and around Madinah to rise against the Prophet and Islam. He became particularly distressed when he heard the news of the Muslim victory at Badr. He took it upon himself then to travel to Mekkah to express his grief and to incite the Quraysh to take revenge. Because of his openly declared war against the Prophet, he was considered dangerous and a public enemy to the nascent Muslim state. It was in these circumstances that the Prophet, who was quite exasperated with him, said to the Muslims: "Who will deal with Kab bin Ashraf? He has offended God and His Apostle" (*Sahih Bukhari* 5.369).

Abu Rafi, another adversary to the early Muslim state was killed after Kab Ashraf for similar charges, and in the words of Bukhari "Abu Rafi used to hurt Allah's Apostle and help his enemies against him" (*Sahih Bukhari* 5.371). We should remember here that even in our modern day legal system, inciting murder is considered worse than the murder itself. These people were inciting murder and violence and therefore were punished for that crime, not just because of their slander of the Prophet.

Ibn Saad, in *Tabqat Alkubra,* mentions two more murders that occurred after the battle of Badr; in one a female, Asma bint Marwan, and in the other, Abu Afak, an elderly Jew, were killed for similar charges of inciting rebellion. Because of the lack of asnad (chain of transmitters) in these reports they cannot be considered reliable. The same is true for the report related to the murders of Nazar bin Al Haris and Uqba bin Abi Muhit, who were enemy combatants captured at the battle of Badr (Ibn Ishaq, *Sirat Rasul Allah,* A. Guillaume, 308). According to Ibn Kathir's explanation out of all the captives those were the only two who were chosen to be killed because of their constant rebellion and abusive language, even in captivity, against God, Apostle of God, and Islam (*Albidaya wal Nahaya,* Urdu edition, Vol. 3:311). Even if I agreed for the sake of discussion that the Prophet himself ordered their execution, Ibn Kathir's explanations tells us that it was done for the general welfare of the State and not as an act of vengeance. We should remember that there were no jails in those days and if they were set free, it was foreseeable that they would have once again indulged in inciting people against the State of Madinah.

Prophet Mohammad neither killed nor incited anybody to kill for personal grief or vengeance. Ten years of his initial ministry in Mekkah is clear proof that despite the worst abuse and torture imaginable, he and his companions never resorted to violence. Even when he became powerful as the head of state in Madinah, he never took advantage of his position for personal scores and vendettas. He always acted for the welfare and protection of his subject people, regardless of their religion or creed, and if certain enemies of the State were dealt with "preemptive strikes," it was with the intention to defend the State and not for vengeful reasons. It is high time that government of Pakistan should repeal this infamous blasphemy law from its criminal code.

22. Mehdi Revealed

(Original article co-authored with Dr. Naseemuddin Khurram)

Muslim history is replete with stories of Mehdis, a mysterious personality who, like the Jewish Messiah, is expected to appear before the end of times. Mehdi-dependent apocalyptic vision has become an article of faith among many Sunni scholars, who believe that the Mehdi's reign will end the age of evil and oppression and bring justice and peace to the whole world. This idea of a redeemer who will restore the Muslim honor is a recurring one, and more than a dozen Mehdis can be cited in last fourteen hundred years of Muslim history, each attracting a sizeable following, especially during the period of political upheaval in Muslim societies.

The purpose of this article is to research the Muslim literature critically on the concept of Mehdi in Islam, its historic evolution and religious validity of "Mehdi-ism."

Historical Background:

Prophet Mohammad (PBUH), who belonged to Bani Hashim by descent, was born in 570 CE in the city of Makkah on the Arabian Peninsula (see the genealogic chart). The Arabs, like Hebrews, are a group of people united by a common language,

Arabic, and do not necessarily require certain genealogic relationship for its membership, as many mistakenly believe. Despite this relaxed requirement it is ironic that Arabs pride themselves on their ancestry, and for them Arab was the noblest of nations.

Genealogical chart; the Prophet's kin

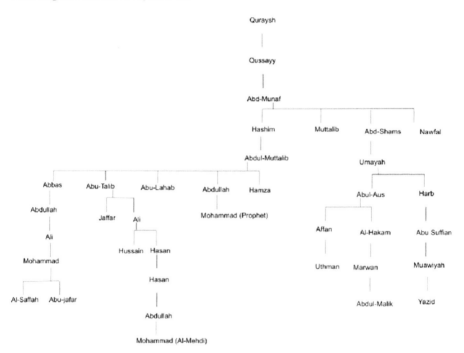

Among the Arabs, the Quraysh, who were divided into numerous competing clans considered themselves the aristocrats of Makkan society. Islam united them into a single body but immediately after Prophet Mohammad's demise the critical issue of succession (Khilafa) arose. A council of elders (Shura) selected Abu Bakar and the title Khalifatur Rasul Allah—the successor of the messenger of Allah—was applied to him. This was shortened to Khalifa (Caliph), designating the rightful ruler of Islam. Thus, for early Muslims succession was not hereditary. The selection of Umar bin Khattab and later Uthman bin Affan was uneventful, too, but during Uthman's time a new political group, Shiites, started to demand the establishment of Ali's

Caliphate, claiming him to be the only rightful successor, as he belonged to the family of Prophet Mohammad.

On international fronts, the Islamic forces, first under the command of Abu Bakar and after him Umar Bin Khattab, started to push out from the Arabian Peninsula. It was during Umar's reign that Iraq, Persia, and Egypt were conquered by the Muslim armies, and in 635 CE they decisively beat the Christian Byzantines at Yarmuk.

Nevertheless, as no change is unidirectional, the Islamic world was rapidly changing, too. Wealth, property, booty, and slaves, which were difficult to imagine in the early days, now multiplied to an extent that boggled the imagination of many. Not only material wealth, but also religious ideologies, including Judaism and Christianity, started to influence Muslim societies.

Unfortunately, at the height of his faculties, in 644 CE, Caliph Umar was assassinated by a Persian slave while he was performing prayers at a mosque. Caliph Uthman, who succeeded Umar, succumbed to those changing times, too, and in the summer of 656 CE, he was murdered in Madina by rebels from the garrison towns of Fustat in Egypt and Kufa in Iraq. As it was the occasion of Hajj, many of the senior Muslims and companions of Prophet Mohammad were in Makkah for the performance of Hajj. Others in Madina hastily appointed Ali bin Abi Talib, the son in law and cousin of Prophet Mohammad, as the new Caliph.

The moral authority of Ali was challenged by Muawiyah, Uthman's cousin and at that time governor of Syria, who later established the successful Umayyad dynasty. Muawiyah demanded blood money and a trial of the murderers. Ayesha (Razi Allah Taala Anha), wife of Prophet Mohammad, led a third group with similar demands. Unfortunately, the rift among Muslims escalated to a bloody civil war and thousands of Muslims were killed first in the battle of the Camel and then a year later in 657 CE when Ali's army of 70,000 faced Muawiyah's 90,000 troops.

Later, Ali, too, was murdered in a mosque by one of his former allies, Abdur-Rehman ibn Muljim. The assassin belonged to a group of people called Khawarij, who declined to accept the truce between Ali and his opponents. Ali appointed his elder son Hasan as his successor, and it was only because of Hasan's visionary leadership that the civil war finally ended after a truce with Muawiyah and surrender of his claim to the throne in Muawiyah's favor. The epicenter of Muawiyah's support was Damascus in Syria; for Ali it was Kufa in Iraq.

After Muawiyah died, his son Yazid became the Caliph. During his reign, the Kufians wrote letters of allegiance to Ali's younger son, Hussain, and persuaded him to organize an uprising against Yazid and to become the Caliph instead. Hussain journeyed with his family toward Kufa, but as he was approaching the city, his cousin Muslim Bin Aqeel sent him a message from Kufa that the inhabitants of this city were not trustworthy people. Sensing their deception, Hussain turned toward Damascus, possibly to make a truce with Yazid. Unfortunately, at the place of Karbala (in Iraq), his convoy was ambushed in the dark of night. A band of Kufians most likely in want of those letters killed Hussain and many of his companions during the fighting. Though Shiites and many Sunnis believe that Yazid was the culprit behind Hussain's murder, Abdullah bin Umar (son of Caliph Umar) accused Iraqis of this heinous crime (*Sahih Bukhari*, Vol 5, hadith number 96).

After Hussain's death, many different politically motivated personalities emerged to organize a resistance aimed to oust the Umayyads from the government. One of them was Mukhtar Al-Saqafi (died 67 AH/686 CE), who was the first to use the term Al-Mehdi. Mukhtar, who initially was Ali's supporter until his group became Kharji, for clearly political reasons exploited the ordeal of Ali's family at the hands of Umayyads. According to him, Ali's son Mohammad bin Ali (Hanfia, died 81AH/700 CE) was Al-Mehdi. Another person, Mughaira bin Saeed Al-Kufi (died 119 AH/ 737 CE), who became famous for his lies and practice of magic (Dar-Qutni, *Zofa Wal Matrukeen* and Zahabi, *Meezan Al-Aitedal*) claimed that Mohammad bin Abdullah, great grandson of Hasan was Al-Mehdi (Allama Abul-Hasan Al-Ashari, *Maqalaat*

Al-Islamieen). Others like Jabar Aljuffi and Abu Mansoor Al-Ijli also shared similar views (Ibn-e-Hazam, *Al-Malal Wal Nahal*).

Another important event during that politically charged environment was the crucifixion of Zaid bin Ali, grandson of Hussain (died 125 AH/743 CE), as he was also organizing a rebellion against the ruling Umayyads. By then not just the descendants of Ali (bin Abi Talib), but Bani Abbas, too, started to develop an interest in the power struggle. Bani Abbas had a sizeable following in Khurasan, which at that time included modern day Afghanistan and part of Pakistan, Iran, Tajikistan, and Turkmenistan (*History of Yaqubi* and *History of Ibn-e-Khuldun*).

After Zaid's subjugation, both these clans of Bani Hashim realized that to become successful they had to form a coalition against the ruling Umayyads. Thus Abu-Jafar Al-Mansoor (to be the second Abbasi Caliph in due course) took an oath of allegiance on the hands of Mohammad bin Abdullah, who was known in his times as Al-Mehdi, and therefore extended his influence over the Shiites of the Arabian Peninsula (*Ser Al-Aalam Al-Nabla* and *Tehzib Al-Tehzib*). Both parties agreed that if they succeeded against the ruling Ummayad, Mohammad bin Abdullah would become the ruler of the Islamic empire. However, once in power Bani Abbas refused to honor the agreement, and thus Abul-Abbas Al-Saffah, the elder brother of Abu-Jafar Al-Mansoor, became the first Abbasi Caliph. Learning of the deception, Mohammad's father, Abdullah, protested to Abu-Jafar Al-Mansoor and reminded him of his promises, but to no avail (*Tarikh Al-Yaqoobi*, Vol. 2:295). Infuriated, Mohammad bin Abdullah revolted against the Abbasids and was given the title Al-Mehdi by his supporters (*Tarikh Al-Mukhtasar Ad-Dool* 108). The Bani Abbas were not softhearted people; they not only slaughtered the remnants of the Ummayad rulers but treated friends and foes alike by killing Abu Muslim Khurasani, Mohammad Bin Abdullah, along with his father and brother.

To us it is clear that the personality of Mehdi was created for political ambitions against the ruling Umayyads, who are now lost in the pages of history. But the vision of a redeemer — Al-Mehdi — is kept alive by the oppressed Muslims wherever their society is persecuted, either by their own rulers or by foreign conquerors. Therefore, Muslim history has witnessed many Mehdis, including "Mehdi Syed Joon Puri," "Mehdi Sudani," "Mehdi Ghulam Ahmed Qadiani," and the famous Shiite Mehdi and the hidden Imam "Ibn Hasan Al-Askari."

It is important to realize that the Holy Quran is completely silent on this topic; neither can we find any tradition (hadith) from Prophet Mohammad in its support, especially in the two most authentic books on hadith (traditions), *Sahih Bukhari* and *Sahih Muslim*. The traditions related to Mehdi are found exclusively in those books that are considered less authentic by the scholars such as *Tirmizi, Nisai, Abu Dawood, Ibn-e-Majja, Hakim, Ahmed and Abi Yaala*, etc.

What will be the real name of Mehdi?

Those who believe in the concept of Mehdi present the following tradition on the authority of Abdullaah bin Masood that the Prophet (PBUH) said, "The world will not end until a man from my family rules the Arabs, whose name will be same as mine" (*Musnad Ahmad*, 5/199, Hadeeth 3573). In another place, we find these added words "whose name would be same as mine and whose father's name as my father's name" (*Sunan Abu Dawood*).

The implication of this tradition is that Mehdi's name will be Mohammad bin Abdullah, similar to Prophet Mohammad's name. One of the narrators of this tradition Asim bin Bahdalah (died 128 AH/ 746 CE) is alone (Mutafarid) in reporting this tradition. Though Asim bin Bahdalah was a trustworthy narrator, in his advanced age he became forgetful and "Mukhtalit" (one who causes mixing of different narrations).

We have already discussed that Bani Abbas in 125 AH took an oath of allegiance on the hands of Mohammad Bin Abdullah, the intended beneficiary of this tradition. Because Asim, troubled with his bad memory, died in 128 AH, I have reason to believe that he might have mixed this event of great political significance with prophetic overtones.

In any case, scholars of hadith have criticized Asim and suggested not to rely on his narrations. (*Tahzeeb-al-Tahzeeb*, Vol. 3:30 and Al-Zahabi, *Mughni Fi Zoafa*)

What will be the genealogy of Mehdi?

Abi Ishaq Al-Sabeei said

Ali while looking at his son Hasan said, "This son of mine will become a chieftain because Prophet Mohammad had called him "Syed" (chief); time is near that a man will appear in his progeny who will have a name similar to our Prophet's name. He will not have any facial resemblance to the Prophet but his virtues would be same as that of the Prophet's. (*Abu Dawood*, Kitab Al-Mehdi)

Here again the intended beneficiary of this concocted tradition is none other than Mohammad bin Abdullah bin Hasan bin Hasan bin Ali bin Abi Talib (Nafs Az-Zakayya Al-Mehdi). This tradition is also criticized and rejected by the scholars of Hadith. According to them, the chain of narrators is broken and there is no proof that Abi Ishaq Al-Sabeei ever talked to Ali (Almizi, *Tahzeeb-al Kamal*).

Furthermore, to keep people focused on the descendants of Ali and his wife Fatima (daughter of the Prophet), and to prevent the possibility of Bani Abbas claiming this "honor" in their family, a few more traditions were fabricated. For example "Al-Mehdi is a reality, he will issue from Fatima" (*Ibn-e-Majja, Hakim, Abu Dawood*), and in another tradition the Prophet is made to say "We the sons of Abdul Muttalib are chieftains for the people of paradise; myself, Hamza, Ali, Jafar, Hasan, Hussain and Mehdi" (*Ibn-e-Majja*, Kitab Alfittan), thus excluding Bani Abbas. Scholars have rejected these traditions, too, because in the first tradition Ziad bin Byan, and in the second tradition Ali bin Zyad Al-Yamami, were known liars of their times (Mughni, *Mughni Fi Az-Zofa* and *Tahzeeb Al-Tahzeeb*).

Nevertheless, once Bani Abbas came into power and their first Caliph Abul Abbas Abdullah bin Mohammad bin Ali bin Abdullah bin Abbas Al-Saffah was on the throne, the concocters of Hadiths felt compelled to manufacture traditions in his favor. Some even crossed all bounds and named him directly as the redeemer. For example, in one of the traditions the Prophet is made to say, "Before the end of times and during the era of sedition and temptations (fitna) a man will appear who will be called Al-Saffah, he will distribute wealth without measure." In another tradition it is said, "Mehdi will belong to the descendants of my uncle Abbas" (*Zaifa Albani*, No. 80).

Will there be abundant wealth during the reign of Mehdi?

On the authority of Abu Sa'eed Al-Khudri it is reported that the Prophet said "At the end of times Mehdi will appear in my Ummah (followers), God will grant him power over rain, the earth will bring forth its fruits, he will distribute wealth to the needy, cattle will increase and the nation (Ummah) will become great. He will rule for seven or eight years" (*Mustadrak Al-Haakim*, 4/557–558). Here again, a narrator in this report, named Abi-Siddique Al-Naaji, was considered untrustworthy by the scholars (*Zuoafa Uqailli* 502).

Will God guide Mehdi to righteousness?

In another tradition, on the authority of Ali, Prophet Mohammad was made to say, "Mehdi is one of us, a member of my family (Ahl-e-Bait). God will make him righteous in a single night" (*Musnad Ahmad*, 2/58, hadeeth 645; and *Sunan Ibn-e-Majja*, 2/1367). Abn Qaisarani has included this tradition in his book *Al-Mozoa'at* (concocted narrations). Imam Bukhari was of the opinion that this tradition is "Mahal An Nazar" (meaning to be taken with caution) as this is the only tradition to the credit of Yaseen bin Shaiban Al-Ijili (one of the narrators) in the vast volumes of hadith books. He also said, "I do not know any other narration from him" (*Tarikh Al-Kabeer*).

What will be the appearance of Mehdi?

It is interesting to know that Mohammad bin Abdullah bin Hasan bin Hasan bin Ali bin Abi Talib was a dark skinned person with a heavy build; that is why Abu-Jafar Al-Mansoor, the second Abbasi Caliph, used to call him "Muhammim" (dark skinned) (*Daira Muarif Al-Islamia*). Precisely for this reason, the concocters of Hadiths reported, "Mehdi will not share a resemblance to Prophet Mohammad" because everyone knew that the Prophet was fair skinned and lean. Furthermore, the Prophet was made to say, "Mehdi is from my lineage, his forehead will be broad and he will have a prominent nose. He will fill the earth with fairness and justice as it was filled with oppression and injustice, and he will rule for seven years" (*Sunan Abu Dawood*, Kitaab Al-Mahdi, 11/375 and *Mustadrak al-Haakim*, 4/557). A narrator of this tradition, Imran Al-Qatan, was not only untrustworthy according to the scholars of hadith but also a staunch supporter of Mohammad bin Abdullah bin Hasan bin Hasan bin Ali bin Abi Talib. During his rebellion against the Abbasids he issued a 'fatwa' (religious ruling) that anybody against their uprising should be killed; therefore his honesty in narrating this tradition is questionable.

Will Jesus pray behind Mehdi?

It is narrated from Jabir that the Prophet said, "Soon Jesus son of Mary will descend (in a group of people) and their leader, Mehdi, will say, "Come (Jesus) lead us in prayer" but he will say, "No, one of you should lead the congregation, as an honor from God to this Ummah" (*Musnad Harith bin Abi Usama*). Scholars argue that Wahab bin Munabbah, the main narrator of this tradition, never met Jabbir bin Abdullah (Al-Iraqi, *Toohfa al-Tahseel fiz Zikar Riwayyata al-Maraseel*); therefore, the authenticity of this tradition is doubtful.

Imam Muslim reported the correct version of this tradition with the exclusion of the word "Mehdi." It thus reads, "Then Jesus son of Mary will descend (among the people) and their leader will say, 'Come, lead us in prayer,' but he will say, 'No, some of you are leaders over others as an honor from God to this Ummah" (*Sahih Muslim* 225). The last sentence of the narration clearly indicates that anyone in this Ummah can be an Imam, not necessarily the Al-Mehdi.

From where will Mehdi's army rise?

In a number of weak traditions, it is claimed that Mehdi's army will rise from Khurasan (*Ibn-e-Majja, Hakim,* and *Musnad Ahmed*). We are told on the authority of Sooban, a companion of Prophet Mohammad, that the Prophet said, "When you see black flags appearing from the East then become a part of that army because it will have the Caliph Al-Mehdi" (*Ibn-e-Majja, Hakim,* and *Musnad Ahmed*). The three main sub-narrators of this tradition are Abi Qallabah, Khalid Al-Haza, and Ali bin Zaid, all considered untrustworthy by the scholars (*Zoafa Uqali, Tahzeeb AlTahzeeb, Mezan Alaitedal*). In another concocted version, it is claimed that Mehdi will in fact be in Madinah, and his supporters coming from Khurasan will make him a Caliph (*Ibn-e-Majja*). We already have discussed the significance of Khurasan from where the Bani Abbas were operating; especially Abu Muslim Khurasani, the staunch supporter of Bani Abbas who forced people to wear black colored clothes and turbans, and raised the black flags.

Will Mehdi distribute the treasure of Kabba?

It is also reported in one of the traditions that Mehdi will distribute the treasure of Kabba (Taj Al-Kabba) to the public. It is interesting to note that during the reign of the second Abbasi Caliph, Abu Jafar Al-Mansoor, this treasure of Kabba has been distributed to the public (*Muqaddama Ibn-e-Khuldun*).

Can we trace Jewish religious influence in the concept of Mehdi-ism?

Very strongly, the answer is yes. Let us first review the following Muslim traditions and then I will answer this question in a little more detail.

On the authority of Abu Huraira, Prophet Mohammad was made to say, "An undefeated army with black flags will rise from Khurasan which will conquer Aelia (Jerusalem) (*Tirmizi*)."

This tradition is narrated by Rashdain bin Saad, who was famous for telling lies (*Tahzeeb At-Tahzeeb*).

A few more weak traditions from the book *Kitab Al-Fitan*, by Naeem bin Hammad, state: "It has come to our attention that the Ark of Covenant will reappear on the hands of Mehdi, from the sea of Tiberius (west shore of sea of Galilee), which he will place in the temple of Jerusalem (Bait-al-Maqdas). The very sight of it will make most of the Jews submissive to God except a few. Thereafter Mehdi will pass away" (Vol. 1, No. 1050).

"He will be called Mehdi as he will instruct people into hidden matters such as revealing the true Torah (of Moses) and the Gospel (of Jesus Christ) from Antioch" (Vol. 1, No. 1023).

Surprisingly, even the Shiites of today believe that their twelfth hidden Imam Ibn-e-Hasan Al-Askari (Imam Mehdi of modern day Shiites) upon his reappearance will give a new scripture and religion to the world and will bring forth the true Jewish and Christian scriptures (*Usool-e-Kafi*, Vol. 4, 444).

An obvious favoritism toward Jewish religious philosophies is appreciable in the above-mentioned traditions. Either some converted Jews brought these ideas along with them or Muslim propagandists against the Ummayad were trying to catch new recruits for their campaign. Although both these propositions are possible, I am inclined to believe the first suggestion for the following reasons.

We know from the Dead Sea scrolls that Jews at around the time of Jesus Christ's appearance were waiting for two Messiahs, one priestly and the other kingly (Vermes, *The Complete Dead Sea Scrolls in English* 84–90). I think this "two Messiah" eschatology was based on the ancient Jewish system of governance where a priest (Zadok) and a king (David), each one acting in his respective sphere of influence, were thought to bring heaven and earth closer to each other in perfect harmony. The reason the Jewish priesthood rebuked Jesus was because he presented himself as a priestly Messiah, whereas they were waiting for a kingly Messiah to appear who could deliver them from the Romans. To them, Jesus was not worthy of the title as he was not enlightened enough to understand the ideology of two Messiahs.

Muslims, on the other hand, believe that Jesus was the Messiah and therefore refrain from subdividing this title into a kingly and a priestly variety as mentioned earlier. They also believe that "Jesus was neither killed nor crucified," that God saved him from the evil plans of his enemies, ascended him alive unto Himself, and will cause him to return to this world before the end of times. Adding Mehdi to Jesus-dependent apocalyptic scenarios has a clear Jewish element of the ancient two Messiah philosophy, wherein Mehdi is behaving as a king and Jesus as a priest.

The concept of Mehdi has evolved to give legitimacy of governance to different political groups of interest for clear political ambitions and has nothing to do with Islam. The Holy Quran and the authentic prophetic traditions (*Sahih Bukhari* and *Sahih Muslim*) are completely silent on this topic. Therefore, Mehdi-related traditions, which we proved are weak, should be approached with caution. An interesting parallel with Jewish eschatology is obvious.

23. Remembering September 11

The region of the Middle East has a unique position in history. Not only did it give rise to such religious ideologies as Judeo-Christianity and Islam, which became the foundation of western and Islamic civilizations respectively, but it has given birth to religious fanatics and extremists, too, who in their respective time periods terrorized many rulers and states to achieve different religious and political agendas. Analysis of these terrorist groups of the past, as well as of the present, makes it clear that there are two obvious requirements to launch a successful terror campaign: an organization capable of launching an attack and a faith-based ideology that brainwashes the attacker to the point of killing and dying.

The first group deserving mention is from ancient Palestine and originated some two thousand years ago. Called Sicarii, or "dagger-men," the group consisted of religious fanatic Jews who conducted a program of assassination against both the Roman conquerors and fellow Jews whom they accused of collaborating with the Romans. They stabbed their victims in crowded market streets and then melted into the crowd. Their slogan "no ruler but God" had a political connotation of belonging to self-professed rightly guided people of God demanding an allegiance from their fellow Jews. Like Robin Hood of medieval England, the group was supported by the peasants but was considered rebels in the eyes of those responsible for maintaining order. The Roman armies hunted them diligently and remorselessly, and it took a few years before they were able to mop up the group completely. Their last hideout was a fortress on a mountain top called Masada, and before the Romans could storm it, the group, with their wives and children, committed suicide.

The second group, assassins, originated when the Fatmid Caliph Al-Mustansar (1036–1094 CE), Imam of the sect and the head of the Ismaili Shiite faith, died in Cairo leaving a disputed succession. The group, mainly consisting of Persian and Syrian Ismailis, supported the elder son of Al-Mustansar, Nizar, who in confrontation with his younger brother Al-Mustali was defeated, captured, and later killed. Later Hasan Sabah, well-versed in Ismaili ideology, became the most ardent preacher of the order and won many converts. Giving the glad tidings of Heaven, trained killers, "fidaees," were prepared, coached where and when to place the dagger in their victim's bosom. Operating from the castle of Alamut in the mountainous region of northern Persia, the group terrorized rulers and elites from Egypt to Persia, and their reign of terror lasted for almost two centuries. Finally, the end of the power of the assassins came under the double assault of the Mongols and of the Mamluk sultan of Egypt.

Readers can appreciate the similarities between the present-day terrorist group Al-Qaeeda and its predecessor Sicarii and assassins. Operating from the difficult to reach mountainous regions of the Pak-Afghan border, the group and its associate organizations have shown the capability to not only attack distant lands such as America but many parts of Europe, too, making them the most powerful and fearsome group the world has ever seen. Its leader, Osama bin Laden, used to frequently quote from the Holy Quran to arouse his supporters, congratulating and giving glad tidings of Heaven on their immoral acts of killing innocent civilians, including women and children, which in fact is the biggest weakness of the group and should be made public on every forum. The American act of attacking the terror bases in Afghanistan and Iraq, and Pakistan's campaign against these terrorists within its border, should be seen with the historic insight that these terrorist groups cannot be negotiated with. The only way to deal with their campaign to "bomb the world" is with stern military action to wipe them out completely.

I think the peace-loving world should continue backing the ongoing efforts against these terrorist groups and hope that current reign of terror will end in a very short time. Immorality has never succeeded in the past and neither should it be allowed to prevail now.

24. "Fiqa-e-America" in Evolution

D r. Ameena Wadud, a female scholar of Islamic studies, has clearly shocked the Islamic world by leading a mixed congregational prayer in New York City (March 2005). Like any argument, there are two sides in this battle, too: one approving her actions as a new possibility and a step forward in Islam and the other seeing it as a "fitna" and innovation in Islam with the possibility of western conspiracy behind the picture. The purpose of this article is not to support one group and refute the other but rather to appeal to the intellectual masses to look sympathetically on Dr. Wadud's actions and try to understand the dynamics of her religious actions before delivering insensitive fatwas.

For last two to three decades we have seen mass emigration, an exodus of Muslims to the United States and Europe for purely economic reasons. Like Jews before them, they have faced unfamiliar customs and social norms in the new land wherever they settled. Overnight they became a minority, losing the majority status they enjoyed in their respective countries. Now under the microscope, they are bombarded with many questions concerning their religion and customs—and a favorite issue is women's rights in their religion. Again, I am not going to write a lengthy discourse on it because logically up to this time there have been only two options available: either to agree with the questioner that women are leading an oppressed life in Islamic countries and close one's eyes, assuming that the storm has subsided, or fight back, citing references of women's contributions in the early days of Islam—and ironically finding none afterward.

Let me confess here that I disagree with Dr. Wadud's actions, but I think she is honestly trying to answer this question in a new way that upholds her Islamic identity, while trying to prevent onslaught on her religion by empowering and distancing herself from the established Islamic code of life. She stated "The issue of gender equality is a very important one in Islam, and Muslims have unfortunately used highly restrictive interpretations of history to move backward" (reported by the BBC), a rather bold confession suggesting that it is a matter of simply misunderstanding the religion.

Let me remind my readers that the four known schools of Sunni Islamic jurisprudence (fiqa) evolved centrifugally, that is, away from Makkah, the birthplace of Islam. The "Maliki" evolved in Madina, the "Shafai" in Egypt, and "Hanbali" and "Hanafi" in Baghdad, all at the time of excellence and zenith of those cities. Even the "Shiite" evolved in the territories of Iraq. Today the seat of learning and education has shifted to Europe and America, and it is quite conceivable that many new ideologically provoking ideas will emerge from these new centers sheltering many Islamic scholars from all over the world.

As the typical Islamic jurisprudence evolved some twelve hundred years ago in a Muslim-dominated environment that assumed Muslims would never become a minority, the Islamic scholarship of mainstream Islam today finds it difficult to answer these new social challenges and if I am successful in conveying what I intended to say, you can foresee that the future holds many surprises for us. To understand this point further, consider another social problem about to loom in west, and that is the religious rights of children born out of mixed religious marriages. Which religion will they follow? One or the other or a one with mixed flavoring? What church or mosque will they go to? Or will there be a universal place of worship for them? And who will lead their congregation? If the established jurisprudence does not answer these questions ahead of time then another radical solution will be sought in future and maybe then we will realize that evolution always finds a way to express itself. Are we witnessing the birth of a new Fiqa in America? Only time will tell.

25. What Would Prophet Mohammad (PBUH) Have Done?

O ne of Denmark's largest selling newspapers, *Jyllands-Posten*, has finally issued an apology (January 2006) to the "honorable citizens of the Muslim world" after publishing a series of caricatures of Prophet Mohammad that provoked violent protests across the Muslim world. In a few of those twelve cartoons, Prophet Mohammad is shown wearing a bomb-shaped turban, looking for virgins with his companions, and guarding veiled females with a dagger. This clearly reflects not just a post 9/11 Islamo-phobic mentality, but contempt for the world's second largest religion, for which the newspaper was rightly ashamed of, either by choice or submission.

But this is not an isolated event we have witnessed here; a few months ago it was the issue of desecration of the Holy Quran at Guantánamo Bay by a few US soldiers, and that, too, led to many violent protests in the Muslim world. As the pattern is a recurring one, we should anticipate similar events in future, as there will be ever new ideas and methods to stir new controversies. Like learned behavior, two obvious patterns of Muslim reaction have emerged so far, and a little discussion is essential so as to adopt the rationally nobler among them. Or do we have other alternatives?

The first is, of course, the typically violent, emotional, slogan raising, "flag burning" attitude that we have seen many times in the past. The second, relatively new approach adopted by Saudi clerics, is to give a peaceful call for economic boycott of the country concerned. In the case of the cartoons, apparently that economic pinch became the reason why the newspaper apologized. Though post 9/11, Saudi clerics with their Wahabi branded Islamic ideology have gained a reputation for intolerance, as many of the hijackers were Saudi nationals; the wisdom with which Saudi clerics have peacefully defended Islam in these perilous times is commendable. Clearly registering one's protest by boycotting is more "democratic" than destroying one's own country and property — an act that does not make sense to me at all.

I learned an interesting lesson from a Christian friend of mine. In 1998 a stage drama was presented at one of the theatres on Broadway, in New York City, in which Jesus Christ was shown as a homosexual. Enraged with the idea, I called up that friend, with whom I also used to have interfaith discussions, and inquired as to his reaction. I even expressed to him proudly that if such thing would have happened in Pakistan, people there would have gone to any extreme, insinuating that our love for Jesus is more than Christians'. To my dismay he remained calm and replied that Christians would definitely protest this, but in America there are many forums and venues that can be utilized for this purpose, excluding the possibility of violent protests. And he was absolutely right, as during the subsequent few weeks I saw many newspaper columns, TV shows, and radio programs all condemning and showing disgust for the idea. Many Christians even called their elected representatives to record their protest, but all refrained from disturbing the civic order. I think Muslims, too, should start utilizing the services of their elected representatives and make use of them and their governments instead of bringing such sensitive matters to the streets.

Lastly, I feel it is important to ask one simple question of ourselves: what would Prophet Mohammad have done if such caricatures had appeared in his own times; what would be his response seeing the Holy Quran is being desecrated? Would he have reacted any differently?

I doubt if he would have resorted to any kind of violent agitations — not even the economic boycott, for that matter — because we know that during the early period of his prophet-hood, Prophet Mohammad himself was constantly subject to offences, both verbal and physical, but his own reaction to his opponents was always a very tolerant one, praying to God to be merciful and show guidance to those who were ignorant. It was his love for others, including his enemies, that actually changed hearts and minds toward Islam. It is high time that we Muslims should decide if we are ready to set such a high example in imitation of Prophet Mohammad, may peace and blessings be upon him forever.

26. Moon Sighting or Moon Fighting

O nce again the Muslim community in North America became bitterly divided over the issue of moon sighting for Eid-ul-Fitar. As a result two Eids were celebrated, one on Thursday and the other one on Friday, the third and fourth of November (2005) respectively. None of us would have objected if the two Eids had been celebrated at different moon sighting zones of the United States because, after all, we are living on a continent that is far bigger than any country we know of, with four different time zones and a distance of thousands of miles from one coast to the other. But the problem arose when the two Eids were celebrated in the same cities throughout the United States, leaving masses in confusion about the validity of their Islamic rites.

The following brief review is my understanding on the topic:

Prophet Mohammad (PBUH) commanded Muslims to look diligently for the moon of Ramadan and Eid-ul-Fitar. It is narrated in *Sahih Bukhari* that he said, "When you see it (new moon of Ramadan) then fast; and when you see it (new moon of Shawwal) then break your fast." In another hadith from Bukhari he said, "Fast according to its sighting and break your fast according to its sighting. And if it is hidden (the moon on 29th) from you by clouds then complete the days as 30." Another narration recorded by Ahmed and Nasai has similar wordings with the added words, "and be devout for looking for it (the new moon)." He and his companions watched for the new moon themselves.

If the moon was not sighted by him or his companions, he took Shahada (witness) from Muslims who were in the suburbs of Madina — that is, a "camel ride distance" away. It is narrated in Abu Dawood that

> Once the people doubted the appearance of the moon of Ramadan, and intended neither to offer the tarawih prayer nor to keep fast. A bedouin came from al-Harrah and testified that he had sighted the moon. He was brought to the Prophet (may peace be upon him). He asked: Do you testify that there is no god but Allah, and that I am the Apostle of Allah? He said: Yes, and he testified that he had sighted the moon. He commanded Bilal who announced to the people to offer the tarawih prayer and to keep fast.

Employing newer technologies like a mathematical calculation of the moon's conjecture, telephones, and the Internet, and taking evidence of moon sighting from distant places within America, and in some cases faraway lands like Saudi Arabia, as our own has only compounded the problem and the controversy associated with it.

Many of us are obsessed with the idea of having one Eid per country and common start and finish dates for Ramadan, and disregard the opinion of Prophet Mohammad's companions who were the first to face this question when the boundaries of Islamic civilization expanded fourteen hundred years ago. It is narrated in *Sahih Muslim* as well as in *Sunnan Abu Dawood* that

Kuraib said that Umm al-Fadl, daughter of al-Harith, sent him to Mu'awiyah in Syria. He said: I came to Syria and performed her work. The moon of Ramadan appeared while I was in Syria. We sighted the moon on the night of Friday. When I came to Medina towards the end of the month (of Ramadan), Ibn 'Abbas asked me about the moon. He said: When did you sight the moon? I said: I sighted it on the night of Friday. He asked: Did you sight it yourself? I said Yes, and the people also sighted it. They fasted and Mu'awiyah also fasted. He said; But we sighted it on the night of Saturday. Since then we have been fasting until we complete thirty days or we sight it (earlier on 29th day). Then I said: Are the sighting of the moon by Mu'awiyah and his fasts not sufficient for us? He replied: No. The Apostle of Allah (may peace be upon him) commanded us to do so.

Imam Muslim made the following heading before describing the above- mentioned narration, "There is a sighting of the moon for every town; The sighting at one town cannot be held valid for the other town situated at a considerable distance from it."

I'll rest my case by stating that every city in United States should have their own moon sighting committee, and we should stop making the moon behave according to our desires of "one Eid per country," which is an impossible task for the American continent.

27. EL, Allu, Elli, God, and Allah

After the visit of Ariel Sharon to the Al-Aqsa mosque in September 2000, CNN broadcast an interview covering the opinions of Jewish settlers living close to the borders of the Palestinian Authority. One of the residents commented on the situation by stating, "This [Israel] is a reality and that [pointing toward Palestine] a prophecy."

The statement reminded me to appreciate the fact that in the Holy Bible alone, no less than three hundred times the word Philistine is used and almost always with animosity and in conflict with the Jews (Israel). Not only that, but the Bible tells us that a single Jew can kill hundreds of Philistines, as is told in the stories of Samson and Shamgar (*Holy Bible*, Judg. 15 and 3).

I am surprised at the convenience with which western scholars find the roots of Muslim terrorism in the Holy Quran and overlook the state-sponsored terrorism committed by the Israeli government. Without going into the details of the Aegean origin of ancient Philistine and their pagan religious practices, it will be sufficient to say that current Palestinians are essentially Arabs in ancestry and worship the same, one, and only true God, variously known as El in Hebrew, Allu in Babylonian, Elli in Aramaic, and Allah in Arabic languages. People should realize that biblical Philistine is a story of the past that has no bearing on modern-day Palestine, except a little resemblance in the names. The area was renamed Palestina by Roman emperor Hadrian in 130–135 CE when he utterly crushed the Bar Koch bar's revolt (second Jewish War) and expunged the name Judea, to rub the noses of the defeated rebels in the Latinized name of their ancient Philistine enemies. To the Palestinian, my message is very simple. If they want to live with dignity, they should change the name of their state to something like Beth-El (house of El) or Beth-David (house of David). They should also change the name of Gaza to something else, making sure that it should be Jewish-friendly according to their psyche. In this way they will be able to divert the unnecessary "transference" and prevent death and suffering of their people.

28. Liberty and Justice for All?

It is in the nature of things that nations and civilizations rise to excellence and then fall to oblivion. The pages of history are witness to this phenomenon, and no nation is exempt from the harsh judgment of historical evaluations.

It is also an observable fact that nations and civilizations can die of many causes, and ironically it is on the ashes of one that the very foundations of the other can be seen. They can be invaded and put to the sword, as India's Mogul Empire was by the British. They can be absorbed by another empire, as the Greeks were by the Romans and the Byzantines by the Islamic forces. Also, because of disunity a formerly great nation can break apart, as happened in case of the USSR and the Ottoman Empire.

But no nation can achieve excellence and sustain it unless it is virtuous in nature, and virtues cannot exist without following basic human rights and religious fundamentals. That is why George Washington in his farewell address stated, "Of all the dispositions and habits which lead to prosperity, religion and morality are indispensable supports." Some may contend that scientific advancements lead a nation to excellence but we should remember that Nazi Germany was among the most technologically advanced nations of its time, but its contribution in arts and science did not save that nation from falling into a moral abyss.

America's strength lies in moral values, respect for human rights, and in "liberty and justice for all." The post-September 11 reaction of targeting every Muslim, and the procedures such as fingerprinting and photographing every Muslim visitor to this country were as unjust as Emperor Nero's persecution of early Christians and Hitler's persecution of Jews and thankfully has been reconsidered in the light that such procedures will only start a new chapter of racial and religious discrimination in this country. No doubt, an angry America might hurt a few Muslims but in the long run these discriminatory measures would have demeaned its own soul.

Made in the USA
Charleston, SC
16 May 2013